# Ways of Belonging

## Rutgers Series in Childhood Studies

The Rutgers Series in Childhood Studies is dedicated to increasing our understanding of children and childhoods throughout the world, reflecting a perspective that highlights cultural dimensions of the human experience. The books in this series are intended for students, scholars, practitioners, and those who formulate policies that affect children's everyday lives and futures.

### Series Board

# Ways of Belonging

## Undocumented Youth in the Shadow of Illegality

FRANCESCA MELONI

RUTGERS UNIVERSITY PRESS

NEW BRUNSWICK, CAMDEN, AND NEWARK, NEW JERSEY

LONDON AND OXFORD

Rutgers University Press is a department of Rutgers, The State University of
New Jersey, one of the leading public research universities in the nation.
By publishing worldwide, it furthers the University's mission of dedication
to excellence in teaching, scholarship, research, and clinical care.

Library of Congress Cataloging-in-Publication Data

Names: Meloni, Francesca, author.
Title: Ways of belonging : undocumented youth in the
shadow of illegality / Francesca Meloni.
Description: New Brunswick : Rutgers University Press, [2023] |
Includes bibliographical references and index.
Identifiers: LCCN 2023007319 | ISBN 9781978835504 (hardcover) |
ISBN 9781978835498 (paperback) |
ISBN 9781978835511 (epub) | ISBN 9781978835528 (pdf)
Subjects: LCSH: Noncitizen children—Québec (Province)—Montréal—Social
conditions. | Noncitizen children—Québec (Province)—Montréal—Psychology. |
Teenage immigrants—Québec (Province)—Montréal—Social conditions. | Teenage
immigrants—Québec (Province)—Montréal—Psychology. | Latin Americans—
Québec (Province)—Montréal—Social conditions. | Latin Americans—Québec
(Province)—Montréal—Psychology. | Belonging (Social psychology)—Québec
(Province)—Montréal. | Right to education—Québec (Province)—Montréal.
Classification: LCC JV7281 .M45 2023 | DDC
305.9/069120971427—dc23/eng/20230515
LC record available at https://lccn.loc.gov/2023007319

A British Cataloging-in-Publication record for this book
is available from the British Library.

References to internet websites (URLs) were accurate at the time of writing.
Neither the author nor Rutgers University Press is responsible for URLs
that may have expired or changed since the manuscript was prepared.

♾ The paper used in this publication meets the requirements of the
American National Standard for Information Sciences—Permanence
of Paper for Printed Library Materials, ANSI Z39.48-1992.

rutgersuniversitypress.org

# CONTENTS

# CONTENTS

# Ways of Belonging

# Introduction

In December 2016, a group of women took to the streets of Montreal. They dressed in white and wore white masks like ghosts to denounce their condition of invisibility.[1] Most held blank, white placards—their missing voices. Others held signs that read, "We, women and mothers without status, work here and contribute to Canada's wealth," "Continue to ignore us as if we don't exist," and "We live excluded and work in the shadows, but we are not ghosts!" A woman spoke through a megaphone: "There is a problem in society, and it's not solved yet. To turn a blind eye is not a solution. We are ghosts in our society, that's all."[2] She paused for a moment, then continued, addressing the Canadian prime minister: "Mr. Trudeau, you can't keep ignoring our messages, our press conferences, our videos. We keep showing[3] ourselves here. Our existence is a fact; you can't keep ignoring it. You separate families from children. You keep doing this, but we are still here. You must find a solution, you must find it! We can't continue to live in fear." In the streets of Montreal, these women made themselves visible through their ghostly presence. They were there to be recognized, to say they had been forgotten. I watched a woman handing out leaflets to people at a bus stop. Her white attire stood out against the colors surrounding her: the blackness of the sidewalk, the blue sky, a green jacket. All that connected to her whiteness was the snow—melting away, signaling the end of winter and the beginning of spring.

Invisibility is more than a metaphor here: for the women who marched that late winter morning, it is literal. For people like them and their families, who lack legal status in the country where they live, life is profoundly shaped by "long-term uncertainty and chronic anxiety,"[4] caught between the movements of hiding and running for fear of being deported.[5] Many of the families I met in Montreal frequently changed address, removed children from school, and completely disappeared from the eyes of authorities. "The word *banish* rhymes with *vanish*," writes historian and activist Margaret Randall about her experience of deportability. "Through banishment or deportation there is the literal threat of invisibility. Not only when the event is concretized, but in the anguish and uncertainty leading to that. Made invisible. Made meaningless. Superfluous. To others. To ourselves."[6]

This book examines life in invisibility mode. It focuses on the experiences of a group that is hidden even among those who already exist in shadows: young people (between fourteen and twenty years old) from Latin American and Caribbean countries living undocumented in Montreal, Canada. I investigate their experiences from two angles. First, I scrutinize the gaze that erases these young people: the laws, practices, and attitudes that make them undocumented, deportable with their families and restricted from accessing social services such as health care and education. Second, I examine how undocumented status impacts the social belonging young people create, both with the subjects who misrecognize them and with their beloved ones, for whom they were never invisible at all.

The concern of this book is *belonging*: the plural and ambivalent ways of belonging that young people carve out in the face of and despite uncertainty, uprootedness, and invisibility. I ask, How do undocumented young people navigate everyday encounters and interactions when they have to hide their status? And how do they begin to relate to their social environment when they might be separated from it at any given moment? To explore these questions, I recount the stories of young people who establish ties across different affective and national spaces, between *here* and *there*—between their communities of origin and the new lives they create in Canada.

The core argument of this book is that we must understand the experiences of undocumented young people as well as the state attitudes toward them as forms of *ambivalence*. I suggest that not only the law but also the lack of response to the law on undocumented migration creates ambivalence—both in institutional subjects who encounter undocumented young people and in young people who experience ambivalent senses of belonging. Throughout the book, we will see these twofold and interconnected dynamics of ambivalence at the level of institutions and individual feelings. At the institutional level, I show how marginality is reproduced not only through explicit policies (e.g., deportation, detention, surveillance, immigration documents) but also through implicit means that I term *structural invisibility*. Structural invisibility refers to norms and practices that are ambiguous, silent, half-written, or whispered and that erase individuals at a social, legal, and political level. I focus particularly on how such invisibility is constructed in relation to access to education: undocumented children are not named in national and provincial laws, and I show how schools arbitrarily decide who is entitled to attend and what documents are required.

At the micro level, I examine how young people negotiate these ambiguous discourses of exclusion by forming an ambivalent sense of belonging. Following their stories, I illustrate both how such ambivalent feelings are generated and why they are central to these young people's lives. I suggest that the ambivalence of belonging enables young people to endure the risk of deportation and, with it, of endangering the affective ties they have built in Canada.

This book thus reflects on undocumented young people from multiple vantage points: the legal barriers minors face, the hurdles to accessing education, the ethical dilemmas around their exclusion and inclusion, and the roles that affect and agency play in a population that is often construed as helpless. In exploring these issues, I bring into conversation different and often discordant voices: namely, young people's narratives and the perspectives of the institutional subjects (teachers, social workers, and school administrators) who fail to recognize the young people. Besides ethnographic material, I draw on interdisciplinary literature from the social sciences and, at times, fiction. I work here as a collector of narrative fragments that together can help us understand the complexities, contradictions, and creative possibilities in the lived experiences of people.

In what follows, I will present the two main contributions that this book offers to scholarly and advocacy discourses. First, it sheds light on the silent and ambiguous policies and practices that make young people invisible at the legal, political, and social levels. Second, it uncovers the complex, subjective dynamics and ambivalent belongings that are central to the lives of young people.

## Invisibility as State Strategy

This book contributes to the emerging literature on the experiences of undocumented young people.[7] Children's undocumented status, many have argued, works differently than that of adults because of their age.[8] The condition of children as vulnerable subjects in need of protection, in fact, clashes with national drives to exclude those who are undocumented as undeserving.[9] These young people, as Catherine Allerton notes, are "impossible children" for whom the state takes no responsibility: "impossible to educate, impossible to be regularised, impossible to be recognised as 'normal.'"[10]

The stories recounted in this book describe the impossible space that young people have to inhabit between exclusion and inclusion. To understand this paradox, I use the analytical lens of what I defined as *structural invisibility*—the ambiguous and unwritten norms and practices that deliberately erase young people from the legal system, denying them recognition and protection. This invisibility is particularly acute for undocumented young people because of their intractable status as both vulnerable minors to be protected *and* aliens to be rejected. The state faces a paradox: it has an ethical obligation to protect minors and abide with international commitments to child rights, but it sanctions them as outsiders to protect national borders. I argue that the institutional failure to recognize young people stems from the coexistence of these two conflicting identity statuses—undocumented status and age. Confronted by this conundrum, the law often prefers simply not to speak.

The notion of invisibility has often been mobilized by scholars and advocates to describe young people's marginalization.[11] However, Jacqueline Bhabha cautions us against using invisibility as too simple an explanation, as both the cause and the consequence of young people's undocumented status. She notes, "Using phrases like *invisibility, hiddenness, slipping between the cracks*, and *void*, it has been suggested that states have innocently overlooked the problems of migrant children and their correlative duties."[12] Arguing against the idea of invisibility, Bhabha suggests that "children do not *in the main* end up without a state by accident or oversight."[13] Many institutional subjects, in fact, see these young people: police, detention guards, immigration officials, and social workers come into contact with them when young people are detained or deported. Bhabha argues, "A better explanation is that we (policy makers and administrators) see but are torn over how to act. We are ambivalent. Invisibility is not the *cause* of child statelessness but the *result* of state strategy toward particular groups of children," she concludes.[14]

To be sure, as Bhabha reminds us, it is important not to use invisibility as a tautological explanation or to believe that the state simply forgot these young people. Let me make this clear: I refer to invisibility not as the cause of an innocent oversight but as the *result* of a *deliberate* strategy on the part of the state. I argue that confronted by their intractable status, Canadian legislation fails to explicitly *call* and *see* undocumented young people. The intentional failure to call these young people results in an ambivalence toward action: a muddle of unwritten, discretionary, and silent practices that exclude young people from the community of citizens.

The issue of access to education, which I examine in this book, is a case in point, exemplifying the ambivalent attitude of the state and the slippery slope of exclusion and inclusion.[15] While in the United States, there is specific legislation allowing undocumented minors access to free K–12 schooling,[16] in many other countries, the law does not make explicit reference to these young people.[17] This is the case in Canada and specifically in Quebec, where I conducted my fieldwork.[18] As a result of their thorny status as both undocumented *and* minors, access to education is ambiguously denied and rests on unwritten practices. This book assembles the different perspectives that compose this denied access: the fear of families, the struggle of young people with daily invisibility, the confusion of school boards with the absence of guidelines, and the ignorance of the Ministry of Education that these young people even exist. Importantly, as I found, when school boards turned a blind eye and allowed young people to enter the system, they did so unofficially: the Ministry of Education did not assign them a registration code, which would grant them a diploma.[19] It was as if these young did not exist at all.

But if the law fails to call these young people, do institutional subjects also fail to see them? The experience of working with undocumented families and institutional subjects taught me that there is no straightforward answer to this question. When we look at different practices, the picture is more complex than straightforward exclusion, and the state, instead of being a homogenous entity, becomes a site of struggle and opacity.[20] As Alison Mountz reminds us, "The state does not contain or enact a unified series of agendas, objectives, or actors. State practices encompass, rather, a series of diverse interests and bodies that are often themselves in conflict."[21] State actors see undocumented young people as undeserving in critical moments—when they are caught during their migration journey or when they are deported. But in their everyday interactions, they fail to recognize undocumented young people at all, as if their identities can be defined only in traumatic moments of displacement.

Many of the institutional subjects I met recognized young people ambiguously at best or altogether failed to recognize them at worst. Many teachers, for instance, were unaware of the situations of their undocumented students because they assumed that undocumented young people weren't entitled to education. They sensed that some young people had a "fuzzy status" but did not really know either exactly what that status was or what their circumstances entailed. Loose threads, legal holes, and contradictory ways of seeing formed the fabric of exclusion: teachers sensed something, school boards applied unwritten rules of access, and the Ministry failed to perceive altogether. Instead of a definite construction produced by policies, illegalization emerged through the silences of the law in which these young people were situated. This ambiguous exclusion from school had important implications for young people's identity development and sense of belonging. In a context where institutions denied even access to primary education, young people had to quickly learn how to live with uncertainty and ambivalence.

A focus on the opacities of the law adds nuances to the existing literature, which has predominantly viewed illegality as a sociopolitical construction.[22] Many scholars argue that the law labels people "illegal." This labeling, in turn, creates an exploitable underclass that can respond to labor demands of racial capitalism.[23] The literature has overwhelmingly focused on the U.S. context, where undocumented migration has a long history of legislation and is in the media spotlight.[24] This book uncovers a more ambiguous array of experiences of illegalization, deportability, and schooling in the Canadian context, where undocumented migration is not presented as a "problem" in policy and public discourses.[25] This is not to say that the issue never enters the public debate. Media have covered, for instance, issues around the validity of refugee claims or the rising numbers of people crossing the U.S.-Canada border.[26] Yet undocumented migration has largely remained in the margins of mainstream conversations and less visible than in other national contexts, such as the United States, where the image of a "Latino threat" is constantly perpetuated by pundits.[27]

This book thus contributes to theoretical debates on migration and citizenship, avoiding the cul-de-sac that sees illegality as mainly produced by the state. Taking migrants' experiences as a starting point, it attends to the specificities of illegalization and to the varied impacts on people's lives—a task that is urgently needed for scholars, advocates, and policymakers.[28] The understanding of illegalization as structural invisibility, which I propose here, does not simply observe invisibility matter-of-factly; it also allows us to focus our attention on the ways state control can be spectral. How through the denial of seeing and the deliberate erasure from the legal system, the state represses unresolved social dilemmas and denies recognition to marginalized groups.[29] Importantly, it also draws attention to the neglected dynamics of ambivalence that produce illegality by amplifying the silent and discordant voices that often go unheard in taken-for-granted notions of the state.[30]

## Longing to Belong

These complex processes of illegalization have important consequences for the ways young people create a sense of belonging. A main theoretical concern of this book centers on the practices of membership that young people establish despite their undocumented status. How do young people create affective relationships in spaces where they are ambiguously included and excluded?

Scholars have highlighted how citizenship is not determined only by the nation-state; rather, it is a feeling of home, "a material and an affective space, shaped by everyday practices, lived experiences,

social relations, memories and emotions."[31] These spaces of belonging
have often been described, for migrants, in terms of liminality. The
concept of *liminality*, originally used by the anthropologist Arnold
van Gennep, describes an in-between stage where subjects are in
transition from one state to another.[32] Scholars argue that migrants
are caught in uncertainty: they leave their identities and communities
of origin behind, yet due to their undocumented status, they cannot
acquire a new sense of belonging in the countries where they settle.
They find themselves from neither *here* nor *there*: they no longer
fit into the cultural group of origin, and they are excluded from the
society where they create their new lives.[33] They are subjects in waiting, betwixt and between, with nowhere to belong. For young people,
who are highly exposed to the hybridization of identities and self-
transformation, this condition is even more acute.[34]

In the field of migration, Cecilia Menjívar coins the term *liminal legality* to bring attention to the gray areas between documented
and undocumented status, such as when individuals acquire social
security numbers and work permits but no guarantee of citizenship.[35]
Roberto Gonzales also draws on the concept of liminality to describe
the experiences of undocumented young people in the United States.[36]
He argues that while undocumented children are able to gain a secure
sense of belonging as American citizens due to their access to K–12
schooling, illegality becomes their primary status when they enter
adulthood, denying them full membership in society. Their liminal
status, then, becomes a condition of hardship and suspension, so that
young people have nowhere to belong and their agency is thwarted
by their undocumented status.[37]

In recent years, however, a growing literature has also explored
young people's resistance to immigration policies[38] following the
momentum created by youth movements, such as the DREAMers in
the United States, asking for pathways to regularization.[39] Scholars
have examined how immigration control does not create only docile
bodies because "where there is power, there is resistance."[40] Roberto

Gonzales and Leo Chavez, for instance, argue that "the liminal and unstable nature of abjectivity is both a source of life stress *and* a condition that allows for the possibility of change, which opens up a space for human action and resistance."[41]

Yet our understanding of young people's experiences remains polarized: subjects are either portrayed as vulnerable, dominated by migration policies, or they are depicted, often enthusiastically, as political subjects resisting these constraints. Two risks arise from these perspectives. First, in overemphasizing the detrimental impact of different forms of power (such as immigration policies, deportations, and administrative regulations), we fail to consider the ways in which young people reinterpret their condition or the individual and collective factors that may ease the burden of state control. Second, if we fuse together agency and resistance, we risk losing more complex, subjective responses beyond the structural forces we expect people to resist and beyond the social patterns we expect them to conform to.[42]

The common thread in these polarized perspectives is the drive to mobilize individual stories as *structural* stories in order to denounce the exploitative logic of regimes of deportation and surveillance.[43] Yet this normative approach may reproduce, even if unintentionally, the myths of the sovereign state: that national boundaries are set and citizenship is singular and complete.[44] Implicitly or explicitly, scholars and advocates keep asking whether young people belong or do not belong—as if there are two clear alternatives and definitive states of being.

This is where this book intervenes. Drawing on feminist and postcolonial scholarship, it suggests moving beyond normative notions of belonging and bringing new conceptual tools to the examination of migrants' lives.[45] It expands our collective attention beyond strictly exclusionary laws, policies, and practices for a more nuanced examination of how subjects claim a sense of belonging, endure the uncertainty of their circumstances, and establish meaningful communities.

I would like to illuminate here more complex psychological dynamics and subtle forms of agency that remain undertheorized in dominant scholarly and advocacy discourses.[46] For instance, what do young people dream in moments of respite when they feel free and loved? How do they make conflicting realities coexist in their lives? How can we understand their experiences as shaped by both vulnerability *and* agency, beyond simplistic narratives of victimhood and resistance?

The stories recounted in this book show young people as not simply subjected to immigration policies but actively coping with adversity. We see how their endurance moved away from clamorous acts of resistance to smaller, more subtle, and less visible gestures. Young people had different and often paradoxical ways of regaining their voices. Sometimes they represented themselves within rather than in opposition to the mainstream society to which they longed to belong. Other times, they created indirect ways of pressing against the limits and opposing deportation—for instance, by misbehaving at school and not recognizing teachers' authority, or by ending relationships with their friends to protect themselves from the pain of separation.

But most importantly, young people established everyday relationships that were permeated by *ambivalence*—caught between the desire to belong and the impossibility of fully belonging. They were here and not here: longing to belong, in a space in between. They inhabited a space outside of fixed realities, moving across different communities of belonging—their families, transnational ties, friends, and peers. I suggest that this ambivalence was not simply a consequence of misrecognition—the ways different subjects failed to understand young people's struggles. It was also a coping strategy that young people mobilized in response to misrecognition by actively hiding their identities and ambivalently positioning themselves in relation to others. There was always the possibility that deportation would separate them from the ones they loved or that people would not appreciate their situations. Ambivalence, then, allowed young people to distance themselves from the disempowering conditions they were caught in and from the suffering of separation. Ambivalence, when actively negotiated, became a survival strategy.

To understand young people's experiences, we need to understand the fundamental ambivalence that shapes both state attitudes toward them and the challenges they are faced with. A focus on the production of ambivalence, I argue, is vital to examine how structures of power subtly enter affective relationships and subjectivities—subtleties that frameworks of domination or resistance often miss. This analytical perspective mirrors the complex legal, political, and social challenges we face as researchers, advocates, and policymakers working with young people.

## Methodological Considerations

The narratives presented in this book draw on five years of ethnographic fieldwork, which I conducted in Montreal between 2010 and 2015. My research, while it developed as a distinct and independent inquiry, intended to add value to a broader four-year study on access to health care for undocumented women and children.[47] This larger study emerged from the concerns of clinicians and community organizations regarding the limited access to health care for undocumented children and women in Montreal and Toronto. Having the chance to collaborate with other researchers and community organizations who participated (and believed) in this broader study on access to health care helped me critically discuss and contextualize many of the challenges of my fieldwork.

Inevitably, conducting research with undocumented groups raised important ethical issues and methodological challenges given the fact that research could potentially expose individuals to immigration authorities.[48] When I started fieldwork, there was little public awareness of the struggles of undocumented migrants in Canada. Establishing relationships with young people and gaining trust were difficult and slow processes. Initially, I approached community organizations in a multicultural neighborhood where many undocumented families lived. However, the few community organizers who were in direct contact with young people tended to protect them and did not consider research a priority worth the risk. In moments of impasse where research seemed impossible, I often questioned my role and ethical responsibilities. I asked myself how research could be ethical and meaningful for undocumented communities.

Slowly my role shifted—from being an external observer to an engaged participant—when I interviewed women and discovered that their most troubling worry was not access to health care but, in fact, access to education for their children. With other researchers and community organizations, I then coestablished and coordinated a working group on access to education. The group involved NGOs, researchers, youth protection agencies, school boards, and institutional subjects. The group had two aims. One was short-term: we wanted to document different practices of access and assist with individual cases. The second was longer-term: we aimed to create more welcoming policies that allowed access to school for young people without status. Between 2010 and 2014, the working group documented and assisted sixty cases of young people denied access to education.

My involvement in the group allowed me to have a more meaningful role through a participatory process that shifted the research question from health care to education. It also meant that I took a clearer ethical stand, and certainly a messier research role, in relation to the injustices that undocumented families suffered. Many community organizations and young people then started to contact me to discuss specific cases of denied access and share their experiences.

Over five years of fieldwork, I conducted interviews with twenty-five women and ten young people living undocumented.[49] At the time I met them, they were settled and had lived in Canada for at least three years. Young people felt their lives grounded in Canada and had established significant relationships with peers outside their family circles. Most of the young people had migrated to Canada with their parents and siblings; only two young people I met had migrated alone.[50] Most of the women I interviewed were single mothers. All the families I met were undocumented at the time. Most of the families had experienced a prolonged state of legal uncertainty and existential precarity. Given the undocumented status of my interlocutors, I took care of ensuring confidentiality and anonymity. I changed names and identifying details including age, gender, birthplace, family relationships, and year of arrival. Before each interview, I received verbal consent instead of a written form.

Beyond the interviews, I also had informal conversations with many young people and families. I met them at their homes; I spent time with them in the park, at the cinema, in community centers, at public demonstrations, at family parties, and at dinners. Over the years, I stayed in touch with them through meetings, messages, phone calls, and updates on social media. Their lives and trajectories have shifted over the years, meaning regularization for some and deportation for others. In this book, I chose to focus on the narratives of five young people to closely examine their everyday experiences. Their stories, while unique to the individuals, are also representative of larger trends in my research.[51] In all the narratives, the production of ambivalence and double binds is central to young people's experiences.

To complement young people's and families' perspectives, I also conducted formal interviews with fifty-two individuals, including teachers, school administrators, social workers, caseworkers, community organizers, and youth protection agencies. Some of these subjects were closely connected to the young people's worlds. For instance, many young people went to the schools where these school administrators worked, and a few community organizers and teachers knew some of the young people I interviewed. In most cases, however, institutional subjects were part of the same ecosystem as undocumented young people, yet they were often unaware of their migration status and circumstances. These interviews and conversations provided background information on the policy context for access to social services for undocumented families and the challenges related to this population. Together, the ethnographic data in this book aim to create thick and deep descriptions of people's everyday lives, revealing subtleties in meanings that larger studies can often miss.[52]

## Outline of the Book

Ethnographies of migration have an open-ended quality. They reflect the precarious legal realities of people and the uncertain nature of migration, which lacks linear life trajectories and clear destinations. This book follows the fragments and uncertainties that shape state attitudes and young people's lives. The first three chapters examine macro perspectives of illegalization: how state actors (immigration officers, judges, school boards, teachers) construct illegality and invisibility for undocumented young people. The remaining three chapters turn to micro perspectives: the effects of undocumented status and structural invisibility on the experiences of belonging of young people.

Chapter 1 outlines the social and political construction of undocumented children in the Canadian legal context in the last three decades—a period during which restrictions on migrants' rights have increased.[53] Through the voices and silences of young people in tribunals, and by contraposing them against the decisions of judges and immigration officers, I examine how minors are regarded both as children in need of protection and as threats to national security. I show how these two images are two sides of the same coin, embedded within sociohistorical ideas of childhood and children's citizenship that mute children's voices and deny their agency.

Chapter 2 discusses how in a context where young people often failed to be recognized, I came to recognize them. By retracing my

research journey and reflecting on my role in relation to undocumented communities, I examine methodological issues and ethical possibilities for learning and collaborating with families and
young people.

Chapter 3 focuses on the specific case of school—a place
that produces everyday forms of social invisibility and inequality. By
proposing the notion of *structural invisibility* as an analytical lens,
I investigate the paradoxical conditions in which young people are
caught and the institutional discourses that surround them. Con-
necting the discordant voices of different subjects (teachers, school
administrators, parents), in this chapter, I uncover the making of
invisibility within institutional structures, which cause children to be
physically present but legally and socially absent.

Chapter 4 invites us to understand the effects of undocumented
status on young people's sense of belonging as they navigate spaces
of invisibility. Drawing on young people's experiences, I show how
young people ambivalently come to terms with their social and everyday lives through a complex dialectic of both membership and exclusion, resulting in a constant tension between invisibility (as both not
being seen by others and not wanting to be seen) and visibility (as a
desire for recognition and a longing to belong).

Chapter 5 further explores how undocumented status shapes young
people's psychological dynamics with *double binds*—paradoxical
situations that trap young people between the movements of hiding
and running, of being invisible on the spot. By closely following the
story of one young person, I examine how double binds emerge and
how young people transform them—an open-ended space for imagining life otherwise.

Chapter 6 investigates the fragments of young people's hopes,
desires, and dreams to examine the force of affective lives. Under
the threat of deportation, young people imagine themselves and
their communities within an uncertain living future and temporary
moments of respite that allow them to endure uncertainty.

The book concludes with a reflection on the theoretical and policy implications of this study, suggesting avenues for widening access to citizenship and social services for undocumented families. Ultimately, this work aims to contribute to a deeper understanding of the struggles young people and their families endure and the consequences of hostile migration policies on their lives.

# 1

# Removable Children

At 6 p.m., the legal clinic for undocumented migrants suddenly became crowded. People started to gather, taking their seats on chairs and sofas disposed in a circle. Next to me, sinking on a couch, a young couple held hands. They said no words but sighed often. A woman, visibly pregnant, entered the room and sat close to them, moving nervously. About fifty people were now assembled, and the air became thick with unspoken fears. Then the coordinator of the clinic introduced himself and encouraged people to speak. A woman from Mexico, a mother of two children, broke the silence with a feeble voice: "Tengo miedo, mucho miedo, y muchas preguntas. Esa es la verdad." (I have fear, lots of fear, and lots of questions. This is the truth.) A collective murmur followed.

Julio, a sturdy man in his forties, entered the room, breathless. As he made his appearance, he began to speak agitatedly. He held his removal order (*fecha de salida*) in his hands. He said he had received it only a few days before. Once, he had had a *rancho* in Mexico, he continued. One day, a criminal gang beat him up and threatened to kill him if he did not work for them. "There is a river full of corpses close to my house," he said, opening his arms as if the water tainted with blood was still before him. A few years ago, he had come to Montreal in search of safety with his wife and two children.

He worked in a poultry factory: "The worst job ever; they treat you like a pig."

After his family's asylum claim was refused, he felt as though he were hanging in empty space, a state that was both painful and terrifying: "I am refused by Mexico, and I am refused by Canada too. It is as though I were on a tightrope" (Es como estar en la cuerda floja).[1] Julio continued, "There is no law for me. In Mexico there is no law, and here neither. There is no law for me anywhere. For a Canadian, the law is the law. For me, there is nothing." He waved his removal order, the material proof of his uncertainty. After a pause, he said, "That's why I stay without papers. You live without the law, outside the law." He fell silent, then quietly went to sit down.

## Deportable Non-citizens

That night, women and men—their families waiting at home, hoping to receive answers—gathered in a room. They had questions and fears about the gaps they fell into. Their bodies moved uncomfortably, revealing their worries. *You live without the law, outside the law.* Illegality—the law without, outside—profoundly enters the lives and bodies of people. Julio describes undocumented status as an empty space in between: gaps created by his lack of documents in Canada and his lack of safety in Mexico.

In this chapter, I examine the legal context that makes families exist in the gaps, without the law, outside the law. More specifically, I analyze the discourses that construct children and young people as non-citizens and removable to a country many of them barely know. Drawing on four juridical cases involving family deportation, I closely follow the voices and the silences of young people in tribunals, contraposing them against the decisions of judges and immigration officers.[2] In considering these cases, I seek to render the living matter of immigration decisions: the assumptions that often establish a denial, the inner doubts that might transpire from a judgment.

Through the dry lines of court hearings, immigration officers sometimes stutter and hesitate in making their decisions or in justifying their moral reasoning toward children. These hesitations stem from the tension, at the heart of the state, between children's best interests and their deportability. We will see how young people's best interests are evaluated against the hardships they would suffer in the case of deportation and are outweighed by undocumented status.

## Between Best Interests and Deportability

The category of childhood as an object of social policy emerged after the Second World War with the notion of children as vulnerable subjects in need of protection and the creation of an international framework of children's rights.[3] Legislation that safeguards children's rights has centered around the principle of best interests, which is the paramount consideration of the Convention on the Rights of the Child, signed by the Canadian government in 1990 and implemented through national and provincial laws.[4] Article 3 of the Convention states that best interests shall be taken into primary consideration "in all actions concerning children, whether undertaken by public or private social welfare institutions, courts of law, administrative authorities or legislative bodies, the best interests of the child shall be a primary consideration."[5]

For undocumented children, however, the need for protection becomes uncertain and revocable. The state is, in fact, faced with a paradox. It is responsible for protecting children's best interests in view of their status as minors. But it is also deporting the same children based on their undocumented status, policing the boundaries between citizens and non-citizens. The state then views undocumented young people as vulnerable minors deserving protection *and* as a threat to national security.[6]

Negative and xenophobic attitudes toward migrants have increased in Canada in recent decades, and migration rules have become more restrictive.[7] In Canada, the majority of individuals enter the territory through legal—albeit precarious—pathways, including those of refugee claimants, temporary workers, or international students. After they lose this temporary legal status, they become unable to obtain permanent residency and only then enter a pathway of illegality.[8] The construction of undocumented immigration in Canada must therefore be understood in connection with what Luin Goldring terms the "institutionalization of precarious status" at the social, administrative, legal, and political levels.[9] Goldring argues that since the 1990s, Canadian policies have shrunk pathways to obtain permanent residency, and they have encouraged precarious residence categories like temporary foreign workers or international students. These precarious categories explicitly do not create pathways to permanent residence or citizenship and entail limited rights and access to services.[10]

The process of illegalization in Canada is thus connected to what Judith Butler defines "state-induced precarity": a politically induced condition "in which certain populations suffer from failing social and economic networks of support and become differentially exposed to injury, violence, and death."[11] Along with the precarity of migratory status, another important factor that has increased the number of undocumented migrants is that in the last decade, the asylum process has become increasingly difficult and restricted. As a result, the number of accepted refugee claims and family reunification applications has drastically decreased. Diverse policies have closed the door on refugee claimants: for example, the Safe Third Country Agreement, introduced in 2004, prohibits individuals from seeking asylum in Canada if they first arrive in the United States. These restrictive policies target groups from specific countries, of which Mexico is a particularly controversial example.[12] Between 2005 and 2008, refugee claimants from Mexico, who did not require visas to travel to Canada at the time, tripled. In 2008, they represented 25 percent of all claims received. In 2009, a visa requirement was instituted for Mexican nationals, and a 2013 immigration reform designated several countries, including Mexico, "safe countries of origin."[13] Refugee claimants from these "safe" countries had strict timelines to claim asylum and lost both the right to appeal a negative decision and the rights to health care and education while awaiting a decision. The Canadian Council for Refugees, among others, has voiced concerns about the need for refugee protection and about the risks of repatriation for refugee claimants from dangerous countries such as Mexico.[14] As was the case with several families that I met during my fieldwork, individuals who have suffered persecution and violence in their home countries are often refused asylum[15] and face the impossibility of obtaining a permanent migration status, which would entitle them to social and political rights. Those who decide to remain in Canada become undocumented and invisible—their lives pervaded by constant awareness of their deportability, their access to services drastically restricted.[16]

The negative attitude toward migrants is evident in court decisions and legislation concerning undocumented children. For instance, the Immigration and Refugee Protection Act introduced the need for decision-makers to "take into account the best interests of a child directly affected" when deportation would have an adverse effect on the child.[17] Importantly, it recommended that the best interests must be "taken into account" rather than be a "primary consideration," as required by the Convention on the Rights of the Child.[18] In practice, the best interests of young people are vaguely acknowledged in the courtroom only in relation to humanitarian and compassionate considerations, and they have ultimately little weight against national security concerns. We can see an example of such a tension in *Baker v. Canada*, a landmark decision that made history in providing juridical guidance in relation to undocumented children. Let's examine this case in the next section.

## Do We Let Her Stay Because of Her
## CANADIAN-BORN CHILDREN?

Mavis Baker came to Canada from Jamaica in 1981 "looking for a better life."[19] She overstayed her visitor visa and became a domestic worker, supporting herself and her four children, all of whom were born in Canada. In 1992, after her last child was born, Mavis suffered from postpartum psychosis. The father, a permanent resident, separated from her and found a new spouse. He did not financially support her or the four children. That same year, Mavis received a deportation order. She applied to the Federal Court for an exemption on compassionate and humanitarian grounds, bringing her children's best interests to the forefront. She argued that she was the main caregiver for her children, who depended on her for emotional support, and that remaining in Canada was best for the family.

A few months later, a letter arrived. It briefly stated that her application had been denied, without providing any reason. Mavis's counsel requested the notes made by the immigration officer who reviewed the case. The notes arrived. "This case is a catastrophe," they began. "The applicant is a paranoid schizophrenic and on welfare. She has no qualifications other than as a domestic. She has FOUR CHILDREN IN JAMAICA AND ANOTHER FOUR BORN HERE. She will, of course, be a tremendous strain on our social welfare system for (probably) the rest of her life. There are no humanitarian and compassionate factors other than her FOUR CANADIAN-BORN CHILDREN. Do we let her stay because of that? I am of the opinion that Canada can no longer afford this type of generosity."[20]

We can sense here the sarcastic amusement of the officer. Mavis centered her humanitarian application on the well-being of her FOUR CANADIAN-BORN CHILDREN.[21] Capital letters mockingly belittle the weight that these children have and dismiss Mavis's plea as unreasonable. *Do we let her stay because of that?* The question highlights what seems to the officer a daring claim. In the rhetorical defensiveness of capital letters, there is only one possible answer: a definitive no. Canada cannot afford this kind of generosity.

Most importantly, capital letters outstrip her children's citizenship and decry their irremediable minor status. Though they are citizens by birthright, these children are considered dependent and removable subjects.[22] Historically, children have been barred from full citizenship due to their alleged dependence and incompetence.[23] Undocumented young people are even more estranged from nationality. Linda Bosniak, for instance, terms the condition of young people who are citizens by birthright yet foreign by their migratory status "alien citizenship."[24] Jacqueline Bhabha has also examined the ambiguities surrounding migrant young people and coined the category of "Arendt's children."[25] Drawing on Hannah Arendt's analysis of the emergence of statelessness after the Second World War, this group includes minors who share three characteristics: they are under eighteen years of age, they are or might be separated from their parents or legal guardians, and they are not citizens of any country because of their status or their parents' status. Similarly, the court considered Mavis's children as not belonging to Canada—their home country where they were born. Their status remained linked to their mother's, their claim to remain in Canada derided as illegitimate.

Yet Mavis stubbornly persisted. After the refusal, she applied to the Supreme Court for a review of the case. She asked to determine whether federal immigration authorities must treat the best interest of a Canadian child as a primary consideration in assessing an applicant under the Immigration Act. The Supreme Court agreed that the Federal Court's decision was unreasonable. In 1999, it stated that though the best interest of the child is not of primary consideration, authorities should "give substantial weight, and be alert, alive and sensitive to the rights of children, to their best interests, and to the hardship that may be caused to them by a negative decision."[26]

Importantly, this ruling did not determine that children's best interests must always outweigh other considerations. Instead, it declared that the state should consider best interests on a *discretionary* basis in accordance with humanitarian and compassionate values. This means that the consideration of best interests is not a fundamental right or a duty of the state but a decision that depends on the sensitivity of immigration officers. Authorities might be sympathetic to children's needs, but the weight, relevance, and even the definition of these needs are left deliberately open. The interest of a child in the courtroom does not call for a certain result. It is a *may* rather than a *must*.

## A Hesitation

In another legal case, *Panchoo v. Canada*, we find a similar vagueness about children's best interests.[27] Yvette and Patrick are originally from Grenada, where they met in 1983. After five years together, they decided to migrate to Canada, where they lived without legal status. In 1993, their daughter Rea was born. Patrick worked full time, earning roughly $660 a week, and even received a valid work permit, which he subsequently lost. In 1994, after falling out of status, Patrick received a deportation order, which he ignored.

Three years later, Yvette was diagnosed with breast cancer. She underwent surgery and had her left breast removed. The illness severely impacted her psychological well-being. She started to suffer from anxiety and struggled to cope with daily events. One day, for instance, Yvette left home without any explanation. She only returned after several weeks. The proceedings don't specify whether her distress had been exacerbated by her undocumented status and fear of deportation. But they clearly state that Patrick took most of the responsibility for caring for their daughter Rea.

In August 1999, Patrick received another deportation order. He applied to stay on humanitarian and compassionate grounds, given Yvette's illness and the family's reliance on his income. Without him, he argued, his family would have to resort to social assistance. A few months later, in December, a letter arrived notifying him that his humanitarian application was denied. It stated that Patrick was already scheduled for deportation in 1994 and that he had to present himself to the authorities on January 21 to return to Grenada. Patrick brought a motion for an order to stay and to start a juridical review of his case. His motion was dismissed without any reason provided.

As a final resort, his six-year-old daughter Rea sought, through her mother, an interlocutory stay of her father's deportation. She argued that separation would not be in her best interest, in accordance with the Supreme Court decision in *Baker v. Canada*. Yet the judge stated, "There was no serious issue here to the extent that the appellant had no standing to challenge the deportation order. *Baker* does not stand for the proposition that a child now has an independent legal right to launch an action to prevent her parent from being removed from Canada."[28]

As the words of the judge made clear, Rea did not hold an *independent* legal right. Instead, her agency to thwart her father's deportation was intrinsically dependent on her mother.[29] Her best interests might be at times considered, but she was not deemed capable to exercise rights on her own. The state took over the responsibility to determine how important Rea's best interests could be. Vanessa Pupavac suggests that the children's international rights framework stems from the separation of the rights-holder and the moral agent: "Although the child is treated as a rights-holder under the convention, the child is not regarded as the moral agent who determines those rights."[30] Children thus have rights, but they can't assert those rights.

Yet in deliberating on Rea's appeal and the case of her family, the judge struggled to decide, noting that Patrick was an admirable person who deserved humanitarian protection:

> Mr. Toussaint appears to be a man who has worked hard to establish himself in Canada and create a secure life for his wife and

daughter. He has a steady job, is a skilled worker and is described by his employer as a dependable employee. He is legally authorized to work in Canada, permission that is given independent of his status in Canada. He pays his taxes, has never been on social assistance and does not have a criminal record. He is described by his church minister as an unselfish man who helps in the operation of a food bank and demonstrates the qualities of hard work. When one considers Mr. Toussaint's personal qualities in concert with the emotional and financial dependence on him by his family, one is driven to ask: if Mr. Toussaint does not qualify for an exemption on humanitarian and compassionate grounds, who does? I also find it puzzling that the Minister appears to have ignored the fact that the removal of Mr. Toussaint will likely give his wife and child little option but to seek social assistance. Moreover, I note that the Minister was unable to offer one persuasive reason why Mr. Toussaint must be deported prior to his leave application being disposed of by the Trial Division of this Court. That being said, I am cognizant that the substantive elements of Mr. Toussaint's claim are not before me.[31]

We can sense the tension in the judge's process of thinking. A hesitation, perhaps a feeling of frustration with the previous immigration decision that she found "puzzling." To be sure, the judge conceded that the decision would harm both Rea and her mother, who had a strong "emotional and financial dependence" on Patrick. But she had to abide by the law even if it would, she admitted, make "bad law": "It is sometimes observed that hard cases make bad law. But this is only so to the extent that a just result can be achieved only by ignoring accepted legal principles. That being said this is a case in which justice and the rule of law collide."[32]

The judge faced a legal impasse. Even if this decision would make bad law, even if the outcome were unjust, there were not legal grounds to postpone deportation based solely on a child's claim. She concluded, "It is with regret, but according to the law, that I dismiss the stay application but with costs to the appellant which I fix at $500."[33]

## Unusual, Undeserved, Disproportionate

The state, as we have seen, does not consider young people full citizens holding legal rights. It is not surprising, then, that the perspectives of children are mostly absent from legal cases.[34] A few exceptions counter these silences. In *Hawthorne v. Canada*, for instance, Suzette, a young girl, contested her deportation order, emphasizing the suffering that return would cause her.

Suzette was eight years old when her mother, Daphney, left Jamaica and moved to Canada in 1992 to join Roy, Suzette's father and a permanent citizen. It was not a happy reunion. After a few years of physical and emotional abuse, Daphney left Roy. She never gained legal status in Canada but kept sending money to her parents for Suzette's upbringing in Jamaica.

In 1999, Roy sponsored Suzette's admission to Canada as a permanent resident. Following her arrival, Suzette lived with her mother, who provided both emotional and financial support. Her father—who had by then remarried and had two children—showed little interest in her.

One day, Daphney received a removal order. She applied to stay on humanitarian and compassionate grounds, stating that deportation would cause her daughter irreparable harm. Suzette was then fifteen years old and in grade ten. In her statutory declaration, she said, "I enjoy school a great deal and am doing very well. My mother and I are very close and my mother is very supportive of me."[35] She continued, "I love my father and would like to keep in touch with him." But she could not live with him, she explained, because he had been charged with sexually abusing one of his stepdaughters. About her deportation, she said, "If my mother is deported to Jamaica, I do not know what I will do. I cannot live with my father, but I cannot live alone in Toronto since I am only fifteen years old. I would miss my mother desperately. I do not feel that I can return to Jamaica because I consider Canada to be my home now." Suzette had no choice. If she went back to Jamaica (not her home anymore), she would never have the possibility to continue her studies: "When I lived in Jamaica, before coming to Canada, my mother sent me money to support myself, money that she earned at her job in Canada. She would not be able to support me if we were deported to Jamaica and I do not know what would happen to me. Also, there is a great deal of crime in Jamaica and I am scared to return there for that reason. I feel safe in Canada."[36] Despite Suzette's claim, the immigration officer did not even mention that Suzette considered Canada to be her home or that she had established significant relationships there. Dismissing her right of belonging, the Federal Court found that there were insufficient grounds to waive the removal order. It argued that deportation would not be a major hardship based on two reasons. First, since Suzette had lived away from her mother until she was eight years old, their relationship could not have been all that close, and separation would not cause significant suffering for either of them. Second, if Suzette had lived in Jamaica before and had close family there, what was the problem with living there again? "Since her close family ties are in Jamaica it would not be a major hardship to return," the officer argued.[37]

We see here how the state denied Suzette's attachments to Canada: her relationship with her mother as well as the social relationships that she had established with her peers. Her affective ties were minimized as illegitimate and revocable, including a bond as vital and enduring as the one between a mother and her child. Inevitably, this reasoning left Suzette uprooted. The decision concluded that deportation wouldn't cause her any "unusual, undeserved, or disproportionate hardships."[38]

Let's reflect for a moment on these latter words. Why does Suzette have to prove her right of belonging on a negative possibility—that if deported, she would experience *unusual, undeserved,* or *disproportionate* challenges? This is how humanitarian law functions: based on exception.[39] It relies not upon a binding system of rights and entitlements but on an international framework that invites national states to make an exception to the rule.[40] Humanitarian law must always negotiate the protection of human rights against "the national order of things."[41] The court can revoke deportation if it thinks that the hardships it causes are disproportionate. Here, of course, a paradox arises. The state needs to allow exemptions for the very hardships that its immigration laws are causing individuals.

Suzette, to obtain her right to stay, had to prove that the difficulties of deportation would be *unusual, undeserved, disproportionate.* What makes this reasoning involuted and obscurely phrased is the use of the negative: *not* usual, deserved, or proportionate. What kind of reality does such a proposition represent? How is negation related to the process of judging? Here, I find helpful the insights of the logician Gottlob Frege. In his essay *Negation,* he differentiates two ways of judging: one that is used for the affirmative and another for the negative.[42] He argues that in the affirmative case, "the act of judging is a mental process, and as such it needs a judging subject as its owner; negation on the other hand is part of a thought, and as such, like the thought itself, it needs no owner, must not be regarded as a content of a consciousness."[43] A negation, then, is a thought rather than a process of reasoning. It does not require ownership. It is already there: a given.

Frege says that in the case of a negation, we estrange ourselves both from the process of judging and from the act of acknowledging the truth of a thought. In other words, we use reinforced denial when we want to conceal a reality. If we revert the judge's reasoning to the positive form, we see that the court had to establish that Suzette's hardships are *usual, deserved,* and *proportionate.* Even for a court ruling, this is something difficult to state without camouflaging its truth.

The appeal court, which later contested the previous judgment, was sensitive to these paradoxes of language. It stated, "Hardship is not a term of art. Children will rarely, if ever, be deserving of any hardship," and granted Suzette the right to stay.[44]

## Alone, Deportable

In another case, *A.M.R.I. v. K.E.R.*, the court dismissed the hardships of return for a girl who had been granted refugee status but had no one to advocate on her behalf—neither her parents nor the state.

Ana[45] was twelve years old in 2008, when she left Mexico to join her father in Canada. Her mother, who had legal custody of her in Mexico, physically and psychologically abused her. In her asylum claim, Ana recounted multiple instances of violence, saying that her mother hit her at least once daily with a broom, a towel, shoes, or a plate and often left bruises on her body. A psychological assessment filed for the claim noted Ana's desire to stay in Canada and stated that her symptoms aligned with post-traumatic stress disorder. Two years later, her claim was accepted. The court did not consider Mexico to be a safe country for Ana; if deported, she "would be forced to return to her abuser."[46]

In these two years, Ana lived in Toronto with her father, her aunt, and her aunt's spouse. However, shortly thereafter, her father was denied refugee status and moved to Norway, where, a few years later, he remarried and had a child. Ana's aunt then commenced a custody application. At the same time, Ana's mother invoked the Hague Convention on International Child Abduction in an appeal for Ana's return to Mexico. Ana's aunt asked to be added as a party to the appeal application and appointed counsel for her niece, but the motion was denied. The hearing eventually proceeded uncontested, without the participation of Ana's father, her aunt, or Ana. A few months later, the application judge granted an order for Ana's immediate return to Mexico. The police arrested Ana at her school. She was deported to Mexico despite her protests and without notice to her father or aunt.

One year later, her aunt filed an appeal based on fresh evidence. Since her return to Mexico, we read, Ana told a social worker that it had been "scary for her."[47] She described only one episode of physical abuse, but she said that her mother was "treating her badly emotionally" and had restricted her mobility and contact with relatives. "She repeated her wish to return to Canada to live with her aunts," the account read. The judges at the appeal court remarked that the application judge made several errors, including the fact that the girl had not been present or represented at the hearing, that her refugee status had never been seriously considered, and that she had been taken by police from school and sent to Mexico without even a chance to speak to the aunt with whom she had lived for nearly two years.

Normally, in proceedings for deportation, a refugee child must be accorded protection under the Canadian Charter of Rights and Freedoms.[48] The Charter requires that the judge assesses the risks associated with deportation and that the child has the right to representation. Ana's case was an exception to this procedure. Even if entitled to refugee status and international protection, the reasoning of the Hague Convention on International Child Abduction and the legal custody of her mother prevailed over Ana's rights.

## Children of Exception

Two faces of the state run through the stories presented in this chapter. The state is obliged to protect children's rights according to international legislation. Yet we see a punishing approach that silences children's voices and deports them to countries that are not their homes. We observe this pattern through all four of the court decisions discussed above. The state revokes, forgets, or does not even mention their citizenship rights. Sometimes, it acknowledges them in capital letters—CANADIAN-BORN CHILDREN—only to deride them for their irrelevance. It considers children dependent and removable non-citizens, their futures in Canada reliant on their parents' undocumented status and deportability.

These two approaches—one that looks at children as vulnerable, the other as "illegals"—are not contradictory, as we might think. Instead, they sustain each other.[49] The common thread is an adult-centered perspective that characterizes young people as lacking moral agency and, thus, having fewer social and political rights. Recent scholarship has highlighted how tensions between the politics of compassion and repression in immigration policies are two sides of the same coin, part of a moral economy that bars migrants from social and political life. Miriam Ticktin, in her book on undocumented immigration in France, *Casualties of Care*, suggests that policing and humanitarianism are parts of the same regime of sovereign exception.[50] They both rest on the singularity of individual cases rather than on a normative system of justice. This logic creates the image of migrants as victims or criminals without political rights or agency.

In the cases recounted in this chapter, we see a similar logic. The state deprives young people of citizenship and leaves them with abstract human rights, if anything. In the best-case scenario, families can avoid deportation on the ground of benevolence. The Court of Appeal can sometimes overturn deportation on a compassionate basis, by reason of children's best interests. But what is best for young people remains ill-defined, an abstract principle in a vacuum. Most importantly, the court considers children's best interests as only one among other factors. In measuring their weight against other elements, issues of national security, or what the court calls "public interest factors," overwhelmingly prevail.

In the courtroom, children's voices are rarely listened to. Even though Suzette clearly stated that she did not want to return to Jamaica or leave her mother, the immigration officer did not take her opinion into account. The police removed Ana from her school and did not pay attention to her when she tried to explain that she had refugee status. At her hearing, Ana was not represented; her voice was missing. This ruthless indifference to young voices is deeply rooted in the notion of *infans*—literally "someone who cannot speak." This idea characterizes a "politics of mutism," the absence of the young as autonomous and political subjects.[51]

Young people become tied to places they may be separated from, following the fate of their parents who fall into the cracks of undocumented status, suspended between two countries. The thin ice may crack suddenly beneath their feet. They are children of exception, their struggles acknowledged only on the exceptionality of each individual case. Their voices are muted, and yet as we read through the dry sentences of court decisions, their absence resonates.

# 2

# Hidden Traces

In a context where families fell into the gaps of illegality, gaining access to young people was difficult at best and, at times, entirely impossible. I felt in search of hidden tracks, tracing the footprints that people were carefully trying to hide. These methodological challenges are common in research with marginalized groups and are closely tied to ethical issues.[1]

Professional codes of ethics consider the benefits and harm of research, stating that harm should be minimal.[2] The negative risks of research include psychological distress, harassment, and damaging representations of individuals and communities. These dangers are acute for people living with undocumented status. For example, interviews can trigger traumatic and painful memories experienced during the border crossing or through living undocumented. There is also the possibility that research findings become known to immigration authorities, exposing individuals to deportation or further stigmatization.

In my fieldwork, I grappled with these issues for a long time. A colleague and friend summarized my dilemmas when she asked, "Do you think it is ethical to document the undocumented? Do people who hide and try to protect themselves *really* want to be documented?" Her questions compounded the quandaries that had long sedimented for me. How should I approach young people, and most importantly, should I even approach them at all?

While we need to carefully consider questions of ethical responsibility, worries about the harm of research can sometimes be paralyzing and may have the effect of excluding people from the right to be researched.[3] In this brief chapter, I will reflect on these issues and examine how I sought to overcome challenges in fieldwork with young people who feared exposure. I will recount how I broke free from simplistic and potentially solipsistic questions about the harms and benefits of research and how I widened my understanding of ethics in terms of relation and engagement.

## The Shadow of James McGill

When I first started my research, I wanted to focus on the effects of undocumented status on young people's well-being. This was part of a wider study on access to health care for undocumented women and children, involving an interdisciplinary team, community organizations, health centers, and hospitals. At first, I identified key informants among community organizations working in a multicultural neighborhood in Montreal in the hope that they would help me access young people. From conversations with community organizations, I knew that many undocumented families lived there. Many women were employed as domestic workers, and their kids went to school a few blocks away.

Yet establishing relationships proved to be challenging. Many community organizers, teachers, and social workers completely lost track of families once they had fallen out of legal status. A social worker told me, with an air of frustration, "They disappear. They change telephone number; they change address! They don't come to see us anymore. They live underground." Others who were perceived as less threatening, like churches and some NGOs, sometimes managed to keep in contact with families. But most of them told me, "Research is not the priority of my clients."[4] Undoubtedly, this approach was one of the reasons why these organizations were perceived as less threatening: they weren't involved in the task, performed by institutional subjects and researchers, of asking questions and recording data. They simply recognized and supported the struggles and needs of undocumented families who were often, a community organizer told me, "in survival mode."

I recall, for instance, when I contacted Jeff, the organizer of one youth center. He was the main person coordinating the center's activities, and he was from Jamaica. When I told him that I was a PhD student from McGill University, he asked me, "Did you know that Mr. McGill had many slaves? He was a colonialist!" Then he looked askance at me: "So are you doing this for school credits? Or for whom?" What he was telling me, through his suspicion, was that I was White, a stranger, and entangled in a colonial history. When I said that I did not sympathize with Mr. McGill, and my research was looking at broad inequalities surrounding access to health care—and when we found out that we lived in the same low-income neighborhood—he finally agreed to allow me to participate in the center's activities. However, when I began frequenting the center and tried to find a way of being there, I found that I had no place and no role to play. "Being there" means involving oneself in the communities one is working with; it is an ethical quest where discomforts and questions are experienced, negotiated, and never entirely resolved.[5] These challenges were even more acute in my fieldwork, since adults protected young people from the risk of being found and deported. How could young people trust me and get involved in research? What were my ethical responsibilities toward them? How should I contend with power imbalances and relationships between myself, young people, and the adults surrounding them?

## Taking a Stand

Things slowly began to change as I broadened my research focus and adopted a more engaged role. The turning point came when George, a member of the Caribbean community, introduced me to community organizations and families he knew. George had completed a master's degree in social science and was interested in research. He had an inquisitive mind and a dry sense of humor. He was not only an essential person who facilitated access but also an invaluable interlocutor who suggested relevant books to read and with whom I exchanged thoughts and reflections as fieldwork unfolded.

A key moment was when he introduced me to Rosie, a woman who was also from the Caribbean community and who led a community organization for undocumented women. One day, she invited me and a colleague to take part in the organization's activities and to meet the women over lunch. We explained to the attendees that we were part of a study on access to health care for undocumented women and young people and that we wanted to listen to their experiences. But it was only when Rosie took over and continued the explanation of what the research was about that I saw a spark of interest in the women's eyes. "We have difficulties in getting health services—delays, access, fees," Rosie said to them. "They [meaning my colleague and I] want to hear what you've been through, what's the struggle of not having papers. We can make our voices heard, make a change for the people who will come here in the future." That evening, I wrote in my field notes, "Note to self: Why am I doing research? How do people see it as useful and relevant? Listen to what is important to them and their struggles."

From then on, I started to volunteer at the organization and met families living without documents. I took part in daily activities with the women. We cooked and ate lunch together, washed dishes while chatting, and spent time with their babies. Unexpectedly, while I was conducting interviews about their health care experiences during pregnancy, I found that the most troubling issue for them was not health care but the barriers to education for their children.[6] With other colleagues, we then established a working group of researchers, community organizations, and institutional stakeholders. Through this group, we documented practices of access to education, and we assisted families in getting their children enrolled in school. In taking a participatory approach, the challenges of access shifted. Community groups and young people started to contact me and request to meet; they recognized that the study was something meaningful they could benefit from. In important ways, my new role changed how community groups saw me. When I went back to the youth center where I had met Jeff, a community organizer from Trinidad and Tobago, Julian, welcomed me at the door and smiled. As we sat in his small office, he took out a notebook and a pen. Then he started asking me about the working group, listening attentively to my responses. He wanted to know about our work as well as the challenges of young people and the perspectives of school boards. He suspected many young people who attended the youth center faced similar struggles, but he didn't know how to deal with them. I was taken aback when, upon leaving his office, he said "Thank you" and hugged me.

Young people also recognized me as a potential ally. I remember, for instance, one summer afternoon at a youth center, a young boy looked at me curiously and asked, "So what are you doing here?" When I told him about the working group, he exclaimed, "That's pretty cool! I bet many people would be interested in telling you about their experiences." I also remember how surprised I was when I received an email from a girl who wrote that she was "so happy to know that there were people interested in studying what was happening to youth living without legal status." She concluded, "If possible, I would like to meet and contribute my point of view on these issues."

## Complicating Research Roles

My research role became more ambiguous. I was not only an ethnographer but also the coordinator of a working group that sought to improve the situations of young people. This double role was unclearly positioned—it was neither militant research[7] nor a strategy of gaining access to young people. The more militant organizations thought my research wasn't militant enough. I tended to complicate young people's experiences, beyond tales of oppression and political resistance. More positivist researchers considered my involvement far too messy. My research did not emerge from a linear trajectory—one where you start with a question and conclude with an answer.

Through my engagement in the working group, I chose to take a stand—a *political* and a *moral* stand.[8] This position allowed me to situate, redefine, and negotiate research in a context of social injustice and to reflect on the political and ethical implications of the knowledge I wanted to produce. In an environment where families became the target of hostile policies and public anxiety around immigration, it would have been impossible to conduct research without becoming involved in action. Other scholars have argued that researchers cannot simply describe the negative consequences of migration policies, but they need to take an active role in reframing public debates and shedding light on injustice.[9] Sarah Willen and Heide Castañeda, for instance, suggest that ethnographers need "to stretch the bounds of academic expression and scholarly practice by 'doing anthropology' not just in scholarly articles and books, but also in collaborative endeavors and in venues more accessible to broader audiences."[10] In my case, engagement emerged not from a predefined role but from a gradual process of dialogue: a conversation between myself and undocumented families, a way of listening to young voices and silences, a way to see fieldwork as an ethnography of collaboration.

## Ethics as Dialogue

In ethnography, *what* we understand is inevitably linked to *how* we came to understand it, blurring the lines between the epistemological, the methodological, and the ethical.[11] In my experience, epistemological and ethical aspects became entangled in a profound sense—opening new ways of thinking about illegalization and access to services. Ethics emerged within a sort of resonance network: the stakes and needs of young people and their mothers, the reflections between the members of our research team. This space of collaboration was helpful in establishing trust relationships with the young people I met, as it led us to co-construct meanings and research objectives.

As my fieldwork unfolded, I came to think about young people, and what makes research with them ethical, in a relational sense: to imagine young people's stories and ourselves within different communities of belonging and interdependence. It was possible to conduct research with young people because I recognized them as part of a wider community of belonging. I could not have entered their worlds without also recognizing the concerns of families and community groups who deeply cared about them. In listening to their struggles, research took me in different directions and unexpected places, shifting the focus on access to education.

The effort in co-establishing a working group thus emerged from a reflexive and open-ended dialogue. I listened for what I did not already know; I tried to understand the hesitations of communities to take part in research and to transform, in response to these, my role.[12] It was only when I attended to the resistance, mistrust, and suspicion of families and community organizations that I could make space for new conversations: a negotiation with myself, my anxieties, my own expectations. A dialogue with an underground world of families who hide and protect themselves. A discussion with other members of the research team, who shared similar experiences and challenges. These conversations profoundly shaped the entire course of the research and altered my questions—from access to health care to education.

# 3

## Failing to Be Called

$A$s the fieldwork unfolded and I became increasingly involved in the working group on access to education, a hidden mosaic of exclusion slowly emerged. Its core pieces were the fears and silences of families, as well as the ambiguity and confusion of school administrators. For undocumented children, there was no normative system around access to education: sometimes they were excluded from school altogether; at other times, they were unofficially accepted.

Take, for instance, the Rodriguez family. Rosa and Emiliano[1] had migrated from Mexico to Montreal three years earlier with their two children, Maria and Elizabeth, ages six and ten. One evening, Rosa and Emiliano invited me and two community organizers to their house, saying that they wanted to discuss the situation of the two girls at school. Gathered around the table, the family had prepared tacos, enchiladas, and guacamole. The girls were quietly playing in their room, and they sometimes peered into the kitchen, overhearing our conversation.

A few weeks earlier, the family had been refused asylum and received a deportation order. They decided to remain in Canada, as returning to Mexico was not safe. But they were worried about Maria and Elizabeth's education. Now that the girls did not hold any legal status, the school sent a letter to the parents, urging them to pay

$640 in monthly fees as non-residents. Emiliano and Rosa, who both worked in a poultry factory, could not afford to pay. More importantly, they were terrified by the letter. It embodied a tangible risk of deportation: the possibility that the school could report the family to the immigration authorities. The family had heard rumors about cases of young people deported from schools in Toronto and Montreal; they worried that the same could happen to their kids.[2]

"What should I do? Should I remove the kids from school?" Rosa asked. "If they stay at home, what will become of their future?" Emiliano suggested, "Perhaps we could register them at another school?" Both seemed resolved to change address and move the girls to another school to reduce the chance of being deported. They asked me and the other community organizers if we thought it was a good idea. We said that the possibility of deportation was real but that there was so much uncertainty about what could happen.

The possibility that school administration would report the family to immigration authorities was not such a remote prospect. In past years, children have been deported from schools in Montreal and Toronto, making families fearful for their own security.[3] A case in point is that of Daniel, a fourteen-year-old boy from Mexico. In January 2014, he was suddenly summoned by the school administration. He was told that his mother needed to pay his tuition fees as a non-resident, or he would be reported to the federal authorities and returned to Mexico. His mother could not afford to pay. Later that spring, Daniel was caught, along with other boys, conducting a small robbery in a liquor store. He had a hearing problem and could not run fast. While his friends managed to escape, he was arrested. Even though he was a minor, he was detained in a removal center and issued a deportation order. He was later released so that he could complete the school year. On the deportation date, however, Daniel and his mother did not show up. They had changed address, school, neighborhood; they started a new life underground. But in October 2014, Daniel decided to go back to his old school to visit former schoolmates and friends. He was chatting with them in the schoolyard when it started to rain heavily. Everyone sought refuge inside. As he entered, Daniel was asked for his documents. As he didn't have any ID, the school administration called the police. Daniel was detained at the removal center and deported to Mexico, alone.

As I ate and talked with the Rodriguez family, the fear of deportability—not deportation per se, but the *possibility* of being deported—was the reality that filled the room. There was a sense of lingering uncertainty in the air: worries about forced return, anxieties about the future, and questions still unanswered. As I was about to leave the house, Maria and Elizabeth ran toward me in the kitchen. They showed me the drawings they had just made, portraying themselves and their parents. Maria, who was younger, proudly pointed to their other pictures hanging on the fridge. Elizabeth came close to me and said, in a whisper, that she was afraid that she could no longer go to school and see her friends. I wanted to reassure her but found myself lacking words.

## The Silence of the Law

My inability to provide clear answers to assuage Elizabeth's fears did not emerge only from the reality of deportation. It also stemmed from the fact that we navigated a fraught territory, where the law is opaque and silent. Regulations around access to education are examples of the ambiguity of the state toward undocumented minors, which wavers between the duty to protect them as children and the imperative to secure borders. In chapter 1, we saw how the security agenda often prevails in legal cases involving the deportation of families. But in the case of access to school, the law prefers to remain silent.

In Quebec, access to school is both a right and an obligation for everyone under the age of eighteen. There is a caveat, though: *free* education is only provided to residents. Specific categories of migrants, such as asylum seekers, are classified as residents and exempted from fees. Yet undocumented children are not even mentioned. The failure of the law to mention undocumented children may be partially due to their relatively small numbers in the province.[4] In the province of Ontario, where undocumented migrants are more numerous, the category exists in the laws and is exempted from fees. In the United States too, where undocumented migration is a long-standing social phenomenon, access to education has been legislated since 1982, when the landmark U.S. Supreme Court decision *Plyler v. Doe* held that states cannot constitutionally deny undocumented students free public education.

In this chapter, we examine how different discourses shape the social exclusion of children in Quebec by explicitly erasing them in the law. Due to their ambiguous status as both minors in need of protection and aliens who should be rejected, young people are not explicitly constructed by the law as undeserving subjects, but nor are they portrayed as deserving.[5] Simply, the law remains silent: it fails to define them as social and political subjects. We will see how this legal gap constitutes what I term *institutional invisibility*: unwritten norms and practices that make young people invisible in the school system, physically present but not officially recognized as *subjects*. To unpack these legal gaps, we will draw on the discordant voices of different subjects: mothers, community organizers, school administrators, and state agents.

## The Shapes of Exclusion

As I listened to women's stories about access to education for their children, the disparities in institutional practices unraveled. When the child had a Canadian father who could sign the documents for school registration, access was often allowed. But when the child could rely only on an undocumented mother, or if both parents were without legal status, enrollment was most often refused altogether. Sometimes the school accepted the child but asked families to pay high tuition fees as non-residents.[6]

Other times, exclusion took the form of an ambiguous bureaucracy. Take the case of Sandra, a woman from the Caribbean island of Saint Lucia. In 2010, she left her home country with Ray, her six-year-old child, fleeing domestic abuse. When her visitor visa expired, she found no means to regularize her status. She worked for a wealthy family, cleaning their house and taking care of their children, in the same neighborhood where she lived. When she arrived in Canada, Sandra tried to register Ray at a public school. But the administration said that as she had no legal documents, someone else had to sign on behalf of her child. Instead, she sent Ray to a private school where many undocumented Caribbean children went, which had lower tuition fees and installment plans. Sandra recounted her struggle in a quiet voice: "I tried to send him to public school, but they said I had to write a letter and that someone could sign for me. But then, the person who was supposed to sign, she had an emergency, so she left then. They told me someone had to sign and write a letter to this person [school administrator]. But they were very nice to me; they explained everything, and they said I could pay for him to go to school. That's because I haven't got the right document that is supposed to be signed. But then this person had an emergency, and I just decided to go to private school. But they were never mean or rude to me. They helped me and explained me." Exclusion can take many forms. An administrator might say that someone with legal status, someone other than you, needs to sign a document on behalf of your child. An administrator politely explains that this is how it is supposed to be; an undocumented mother cannot exercise her parental responsibility to secure education for her child. Words so polite that the truth, whatever it might be, is enshrouded in the fear of even asking, How could this be? A polite explanation that crafts—so subtly, so violently—the contours of the status quo in the absence of further questions.

## The Opacity of Rights

Sandra's example highlights the bureaucratic haze that deprives children of their right to education. Scholars have described different forms of *bureaucratic disentitlement*: "the insidious process by which administrative agencies deprive individuals of their statutory entitlements and infringe on their constitutional rights."[7] Practices of bureaucratic disentitlement include "withholding information, providing misinformation, isolating applicants, and requiring extraordinary amounts of documentation," which prevent the transformation of statutory rights into tangible benefits.[8]

But in the case of Sandra, bureaucratic procedures do not simply withhold or conceal evidence. The information is not even there. Undocumented children are left only with abstract rights (for *all* children) but without statutory rights because there are no formal rules or laws for their situation. Their entitlements become clouded in the fog of misinformation, confusion, and fear. All the stories recounted by families had this common thread of opacity. Both school administrations and families were uncertain about which documents were needed and what the policy said exactly. While most schools required valid immigration documents, some requested only a birth certificate as a proof of identity.[9]

This disparity of practices, coupled with the fear of exposing their status to the authorities, increased uncertainty for many families. For instance, Marlene, a woman from Jamaica who had lived without legal status for many years, sent her son Billy to school only when he was eight years old. When she asked the school to register her child, she was told that she had to pay tuition fees. She consulted the school board and received the same answer. Her friends in the

Caribbean community confirmed that this was how it was: Billy could not access free education. She said, "This is what everybody told me. You need to have all the documents, he cannot go to school." Years later, when she had regularized her status, Marlene learned that policies seemed to state the opposite of what she was told: "When I finally got my status and I went to immigration, they asked me whether my nine-year-old child went to school when we did not have papers. I said no. And immigration asked, Why? And then said, 'Because at a certain age, under eighteen years old, he doesn't need a study permit to go to school; he *has* to go to school.' But I didn't know that! That's the thing: you need to be informed and know stuff. And when I went to the school, they just told me that they didn't want to take him. So they need to inform the school about that stuff too! Because at the school, they asked me for a study permit although he didn't need it. And if you don't have papers, then you have to pay fees. And they charge like crazy! I don't even remember how much it was because it was crazy—thousands of dollars. It was crazy; I couldn't pay that price!" Here we can see the conundrum of the law. Immigration authorities told Sandra that her son didn't need a study permit; *he had to go to school*. This is what the Quebec Education Act says: every child has the right to education. And yet the school and her community believed the opposite: Billy can't go to school. It is an abstract right, as opposed to the actual impossibility of *can't*. Rights often have the fleeting substance of social ideals, but people know intimately how little they count for on the ground, when caught in the unwritten practices, half-said words, and polite explanations that craft the boundaries of exclusion.

In other cases, illegalization showed its scornful face only after young people had completed their studies. For instance, Samuel, an eighteen-year-old originally from Jamaica, could attend school without paying fees. But to his surprise, he discovered he could not get his final diploma, which would enable him to pursue higher education.[10]

He was never officially registered at the school. Because he was undocumented, he could not be issued the lifetime code assigned by the Ministry of Education to all students that would allow his credits to be recognized and the diploma to be issued. "You are not credited. Even though you are studying for five years and even though you are passing all the courses," his mother said. Then she added, "He is now going into adult education. But it's a burden to then have to take other courses because of the government." Samuel was in school with his classmates, but his presence was marked by disappearance, as if he had never been there.

Young people like Samuel were situated in a space of social and legal invisibility. They were physically present in the school system, yet not officially recognized. Policies of invisibility excluded undocumented young people by erasing their existence as social and legal subjects. To understand how this exclusion works, we first need to understand how the law "calls" us to be certain kinds of subjects, with consequent entitlement or exclusion from rights.

## A Diversion on Interpellation

We are, Judith Butler suggests, "interpellated kinds of beings, dependent on the Other in order to be."[11] Our social existence depends on the possibility of being called not only as individuals but as *subjects*. We are assigned a position in society through both the act of being called and the gesture of responding to this call.

Louis Althusser provides a vivid example that can help us better understand what it means to be interpellated.[12] Let's imagine a police officer who hails an individual in the street: "Hey, you there!" The person turns, an automatic bodily reflex. And in this 180-degree conversion, the person becomes a subject.[13] It is in this circular movement—a police officer who calls, someone who responds to the call—that we become legible and recognized in society. According to

Althusser, the ability of the state to interpellate individuals encapsulates them in the structure of capitalistic economy. It makes them subject to labor and class rule.[14]

Oppressive ways of calling and defining subjects thus constitute a form of "subjection"—that is, "the process of becoming subordinated by power as well as the process of becoming a subject."[15] This is the paradox: power both *subjugates* and *makes* subjects.[16] It makes people vulnerable to exploitation while also making them exist in a social and political sense.

Of course, modes of recognition depend on who is calling us and how—whether it is our lover, our parent, or a police officer. What interests us here are coercive and hateful forms of speech: racist ways of labeling others.[17] In *The Souls of Black Folk*, W. E. B. Du Bois asks, "How does it feel to be a Problem?"[18] He invites us to think about what it meant for Black Americans to be constantly interpellated, in White society, as problems that need to be dealt with. Subjection has been understood in different ways in critical theory: for instance, as interpellation, in Althusser's terms; as a discursive historical productivity, in Foucault's view; as the racist construction of people as problems, in Du Bois's perspective; or as a performative act, in Butler's account.[19] What these perspectives share is the view that people are *made up*: they inhabit their subject position through being labeled.[20] It is a language of making: subjects are manufactured, social spaces are infused with power, laws become edifices.

## The Making of Illegality

Drawing on these conceptual frameworks, migration scholars have overwhelmingly focused on the *making* of undocumented status. That is, they have analyzed illegality as a sociopolitical construction that is strategically created by policies and state practices.[21] The law, they argue, marks people as "illegal," and in turn, this labeling creates an underclass of exploitable people who can respond to labor demand.[22]

Ruben Andersson, for instance, defines as the "illegality industry" the economy of the borderlands between Africa and Europe: "The system in which illegal migration is both controlled and produced."[23] Adopting a grammar of making, he examines how "illegality is not just produced, but it is also productive. As a 'problem' to be solved, it sparks new security 'solutions,' NGO projects, professional networks, activist campaigns, and journalistic and academic engagements."[24]

In a similar vein, Nicholas De Genova calls for a social and historical analysis of the processes of illegalization. He argues that "illegalities are constituted or regimented by the law—directly, explicitly, in a manner that presumes to be more or less definitive (albeit not without manifold ambiguities and indeterminacies, always manipulable in practice) and with a considerable degree of calculated deliberation."[25]

Let's return to the case of undocumented young people in Quebec. To understand their exclusion, we cannot simply rely on the understanding of illegality as a definitive construction, directly and explicitly regimented by the state. Instead, I suggest that we need to take seriously into account what De Genova puts in parentheses in the text quoted above: "The manifold ambiguities and indeterminacies of the law, always manipulable in practice."[26] While parentheses can sometimes clarify or even emphasize a statement, here they have a different function. They both acknowledge and minimize the existence of something that doesn't coherently fit and may even unsettle our main argument. They denote something we try to keep at bay—dormant between parentheses, or in a footnote.[27] While the production of illegality is often recognized by scholars, the ambiguities of the law as well as the leeway of state agents and subjects remain undertheorized.

Here, I would like to take a critical distance from reifying notions of the state and illegality, which are often taken for granted as entities that reproduce themselves. I argue that the dominant focus on the productive conditions of illegality risks impoverishing our conceptual framework and our language for understanding different forms of subjection. When we encounter power structures on the ground, from the point of view both of the state and of the people who are subjects of power, subjection can take more ambiguous and elusive forms. There is, for instance, the possibility that we might not be called at all, as happens in the case of young people. To them, the policeman does not shout, "Hey, you there!" Sometimes he sees the child yet turns away his gaze. But more often, the authority has not even *seen* the child. Never encountered one; never thought she existed. The entire apparatus of laws and practices deletes the chances of an encounter. Because of the contradictory social status of undocumented minors, the state pushes aside the question of recognition, leaving it to the fears of families, the silence of teachers, the judgment of school administrators.

## Saying and Not Saying

This ambivalent state attitude was evident in my conversations with teachers or school administrators. Many were bewildered and failed to acknowledge the presence of undocumented students in their classes. Others, recognizing the reality of undocumented families, lowered their voices, blending into invisibility.

I remember, for instance, an encounter with Richard, the pastor of a small church in the suburbs of Montreal. He helped run a private school attended by many undocumented Caribbean young people. He agreed to meet me in the evening, after school activities had ended. He greeted me warmly and invited me to sit in a corner. It was silent all around us; the rooms were dark and empty. A sense of words unspoken hung in the air. I asked if he knew of any children who faced difficulties accessing education. He looked at me for a moment and brought his face close to mine. His voice lowered, becoming a whisper—even more of a whisper because we were alone in the room, and nobody could possibly have overheard us. He said, "Yes, I see what you are saying. We know these situations."

Reflecting later, I realized that the pastor's whispering was not simply an instinctive gesture to protect the families he had befriended. His whisper—an intimate way of speaking and not speaking—was the counterpart of young people's invisibility, their ways of being and not being. The fragile yet powerful relationships that families established with others entailed a sense of unspoken uncertainty. Connections with institutional subjects could be revoked at any moment, if families felt that they were in danger of being deported. As we saw in chapter 2, many teachers, social workers, and community organizers lost track of families once they had fallen out of status. But most of the time, the recognition of young people was situated within an unspoken ambivalence.

Take, for instance, my first meeting with Joanna, a teacher who talked about her students with affection, emphasizing how much she cared for them. After a friendly chat and a cup of coffee, I tried to get to the point. I asked her if any of her students were without legal status. She looked surprised and said, "Of course not; undocumented children cannot go to school!" I then rephrased my question, asking her hesitantly if she perhaps knew of any children who had fuzzy migratory status (*un statut flou*). She paused for a moment and quietly said, "Oh, yes. I know some."

Her contradictory statement reveals not only the confusion surrounding access to education but also, more profoundly, a failure of recognition. Bounded by the unclarity of policies and the assumption that undocumented children cannot go to school, teachers rarely asked young people about their legal circumstances. Young people, in turn—afraid of being deported and of being removed from school—didn't disclose their status. The ambiguity of policies produced, in the relationships between young people and institutional subjects, what Gayatri Chakravorty Spivak calls a "secret encounter": an ethical engagement characterized on both sides by "the sense that something has not got across"[28] and by the insistent yet impossible desire to reveal the secret. To a certain extent, their lack of status prevented young people from revealing that secret, from disclosing fully who they were. Subjects they met in their everyday lives failed to listen for their voices and—perhaps more importantly—their silences and whispers. They failed to account for what these young people could not possibly say.

## The Denial of Seeing

This opacity of institutional practices slowly started to unfold when, with other colleagues and community organizations, I established and coordinated a working group on access to education. As we saw in chapter 2, the initiative emerged, in important ways, from a participatory approach. The process of listening to the concerns of undocumented mothers was a turning point and shifted the research focus from access to health care to education—an issue that I had not initially planned to study or even realized to be relevant. This new issue, which is inextricably linked to young people's and their families' well-being, reoriented the study.

The working group initially comprised community organizations and a legal clinic serving migrants with precarious status. After six months, it was enlarged to include representatives of school boards, youth protection agencies, and the Ministry of Education.[29] The aims were to document cases of denied access to education, to help families on an individual basis enroll their children,[30] and to move institutions toward policy change. In this new space, different voices, which had been silent or alone, started to come together.

To my surprise, I discovered that for the Ministry of Education, the legal vacuum had created the impression that the problem did not exist at all. Claude, a Ministry representative, was an active participant in the working group.[31] He was a man in his mid-thirties, approachable and friendly. He often came to the meetings with his rucksack and bike helmet. When he joined the group, he initially tended to minimize not only the proportion and impact of undocumented migration but even its existence. There was no mention of these children in the law, he said, and the issue was never brought to the Ministry's attention by schools or school boards. Later, when he became attuned to the different experiences of school boards and community organizations, he acknowledged the existence of the issue. At one meeting, he expressed surprise, saying, "We have never perceived the situation as real." In the higher echelons of the Ministry, it was as if these children did not exist at all.

## School Boards and the Burden of Reality

While undocumented children were not perceived as a reality by the Ministry, they were real enough for school boards. Paul, the director of one of the main boards, summarized this impasse: "There is a juridical void for undocumented children. We need rules that are really clear because the law is not clear." Without any guidelines or support from the Ministry, he felt he was left with a huge responsibility—that of deciding who should have access to school.

Undocumented children were perceived as an unspoken dilemma. Each school board and school adopted different administrative procedures. They decided which documents to ask for and which children to accept. Importantly, these practices were not official or fully written, nor were they consistently applied.[32] Melanie, who worked for a small school board, said, "There is a great disparity of practices, and we don't know what others are doing. We had cases where children without papers did not attend school. We can, of course, use the law saying that they should go to school, but then the choice is upon the school. . . . So we can't do much." Like many of her colleagues, Melanie acknowledged that these children were entitled to education. But in the impossibility of anchoring this right in practice, she shifted responsibility to others: to schools for implementing different practices, to the Ministry of Education for not providing clear direction, to families for not regularizing their status.

For school boards, undocumented status seemed a knot they could not unravel. This became clear during one meeting. Paul explained his position thus: "International students, we ask to pay fees. Undocumented students, we ask to regularize their documents so that they don't need to pay the fees." He continued, "The Ministry of Education asks us the fees for these students. Now, for instance, we have a case of a child from Mexico. He has been refused asylum, but we have registered the child in school. But we call the family to make sure that they take all the steps to regularize their status."

At his words, Maria, a member of a Latin American organization, spoke out. She said that families found themselves with no practical way to regularize their status and that the lack of documents was an inescapable part of their lives. Paul looked at her with a helpless expression. Then he quietly said, "We do what we can to respect the law. I say to the parents, your responsibility is to find the documents so that you can register your child in school and have free education." Confronted with Maria's perspective, Paul maintained calm aloofness. His words became repetitive, uttered in an impassive tone, estranged from the social and emotional realities of families. He failed both to acknowledge Maria's standpoint and to take responsibility. He could only reiterate his request to amend what did not fit the law: *your responsibility is to find the documents.* He couldn't locate any solution for what existed outside the law or any way to connect with the struggles of young people.

We can see how Paul followed here a bureaucratic way of proceeding. He based his reasoning on rules rather than on relationships and ethical values.[33] But in the absence of clear and written regulations, Paul's attitude laid the ground for practices of institutional invisibility. He repeated, "We do what we can do to respect the law." He clearly did not refer here to the Quebec Education Act, which states that every child has to go to school. Instead, he was setting as "law" arbitrary and ambiguous benchmarks of deservingness. It was a gesture similar to the bureaucrat who kindly explained to Sandra that her child couldn't go to school, that this was how it was supposed to be. These ambiguous discourses created unwritten norms that made students invisible. The responsibility of access to education, then, entirely fell onto families and young people. It was their duty to regularize their status if they wanted to exist as subjects.

## Unraveling Invisibility

The working group created a space where the voices of women, NGOs, and school boards converged. It uncovered how at the core of denied access, there was no certain discursive reality but a juridical void: the law stated the right to school for all minors yet also prohibited free education for non-residents. In this vacuum, young people became invisible in a social and legal sense. Sometimes entirely excluded from education, other times unofficially accepted. Even when they managed to enroll, they could not be issued permanent codes from the Ministry of Education. Julie, a school board director, described this paradox thus: "We cannot produce a permanent code because this child does not administratively exist. Without a permanent code, you don't exist."

To be sure, we can't naively think that the law simply forgot about these young people. Legal black holes, as well as discretionary practices, are political strategies. The law *deliberately* avoided seeing young people due to their contradictory position as both minors and undocumented. The process of illegalization emerged from what I term *structural invisibility*, a social and legal erasure that is instituted by the state through legal gaps, unwritten policies, and unspoken and arbitrary practices that ultimately deny recognition and rights. A distorted glass, made of ambiguous discourses and silences, confined undocumented young people as invisible students—an unresolved ethical dilemma for national policies. Invisibility took the form of a school administrator saying politely that your child could not go to school, that this was how it was supposed to be. It was found in

the contradictory information families received and in their paralyzing fear of posing further questions. It materialized in the absence of
an official diploma for Samuel despite all his years in school. It was
situated in the silence of school boards, the discrepancies in their
practices, and ultimately their refusal to see.

Many scholars have paid attention to how frontline workers use
discretion in their daily work, assessing who is deserving or undeserving of services.[34] In his book *Street-Level Bureaucracy: Dilemmas
of the Individual in Public Services*, Michael Lipsky refers to frontline
workers as "street-level bureaucrats": state agents who "daily inter-
act with [citizens] and have wide discretion over the dispensation
of benefits or allocation of public sanctions."[35] Lipsky argues that
discretion—workers' freedom in implementing policies and exercising choice—is a core part of the functioning of the state. While
policies are prescriptive, individuals present complex challenges and
needs that policies can't entirely predict.[36]

This literature on discretion is helpful to understand the myr-
iad of practices that compose what we broadly call the "state." Yet it
often focuses on individual micro-practices and identifies discretion
as the main site of opacity, often contraposed to the clarity of written
legal frameworks. My effort here is to open a dialogue between top-
down approaches that emphasize the role of institutions in making
law and bottom-up perspectives that locate frontline workers as the
main producers of policy. I understand here the state as a concrete
and situated field where both institutions and their actors are animated by explicit and covert interests and divided by tensions and
contradictions.[37] In the case of undocumented families in Canada,
discretion did not only emerge from the degree of workers' individual
autonomy. It also originated from the opacity and silences of policy
and from the deliberate act of erasing undocumented young people
from the legal system.

Importantly, what I term *structural invisibility* is related not
only to the specific context of undocumented migration or to the

paradoxical status of young people. More widely, it is related to processes of marginalization and racialization of groups of people that are cast out of society, in a legal and social void. Achille Mbembe suggests that migrants, refugees, and asylum seekers "can present themselves to us in a physical and tactile, concrete way, while remaining in ghostly absence in a similarly concrete void."[38] He argues that it is "the matrix of their being, of which we suppose they are merely the mask, that plunges us into a state of agitation and radical uncertainty."[39]

We can find a powerful description of this kind of invisibility in the novel *Invisible Man*, written by Ralph Ellison in 1952. The protagonist, who remains unnamed throughout the whole story, is a Black man living in a small U.S. Southern town. He tells us about his life: "I am an invisible man. No, I am not a spook like those who haunted Edgar Allan Poe; nor am I one of your Hollywood-movie ectoplasms. I am a man of substance, of flesh and bone, fiber and liquids—and I might even be said to possess a mind."[40] The reason for his invisibility had to be found, he says, in the failure of people to *see* him. "That invisibility to which I refer occurs because of a peculiar disposition of the eyes of those with whom I come in contact. A matter of the construction of their inner eyes, those eyes with which they look through their physical eyes upon reality."[41] Born in Oklahoma in 1914, Ellison intimately knew what it meant to be Black in the segregated South—how racial discrimination made people disappear. He wrote *Invisible Man* from the perspective of a man who tells his life story in the first person and remains unnamed throughout the whole story. In our inability to call him by name, the narrator shows us his anonymous condition. He tells us about his life as an invisible man: society is blind to his existence as a subject, as a human. Invisibility relates to how the dominant White gaze makes reality and how this reality fails to include people of color.

In the case of undocumented young people, I argue that the production of invisibility is *structural* and *deliberate*: it is a state strategy embedded in social and political conditions rather than merely applied to individual practices and institutional cultures. The analytical lens of institutional invisibility, I argue, can help us understand not only how subjects are produced by policy as "other" but how they are erased from institutional and social settings.[42] Importantly, the analytical lens of structural invisibility can alter traditional ways of describing subjection and its effects on people's lives, assigning a central position to what was shafted into parentheticals: the gaps and opacities of the law and how these are negotiated on the ground.[43] This shift of perspective means not only to pay attention to how policies make subjects but to account for how individuals are made invisible through ambiguous practices and relational modes. New questions open in front of us. For instance, how do the ambiguities of the law make people subject to power? How are legal gaps interpreted and manipulated by state agents? What effects do they have on the psychic and everyday lives of people? From this perspective, the opacity of the law is not simply a nuance or a diminished, incomplete version of a full discursive production. Rather, it constitutes a different political strategy into itself—one that crafts exclusion by repressing social dilemmas and avoiding the thorny issue of recognition.

# 4

## Getting Used to Here

I met Alicia, a young girl from Jamaica, at the youth community center where she went every day. She was fifteen years old, with a bright smile and a contagious laugh. She was inseparable from Jasna, her best friend who was around the same age. Alicia had migrated to Canada in 2008 with her mother and her younger sister. Her father had left the family and remarried; Alicia and her sister had long since lost contact with him. Her mother supported the two girls and worked in a care home for the elderly. She wanted to provide a better future for her daughters but had no means to secure legal status. A few months after I met Alicia, her family received a deportation order. Alicia stopped going to school and estranged herself from everyone—her friends, her boyfriend, her peers. She shared her worries only with Jasna and Tim, a youth worker at the community center.

One day, I received a phone call from Tim. He was concerned about Alicia and asked me to convince her to stay in school. Alicia agreed to meet us the following week, but when I arrived at the meeting place, she was not there. Tim tried to call her; she didn't answer. He tried to call her boyfriend Luke; he did not know where Alicia was. Half an hour later, Alicia sent us a text: "OMG I'm so sorry!!! Had a problem with my mom, I'm coming!!!" She finally arrived, out of breath. "I am sooo sorry; I had a big argument with my mom!" she said. She seemed scattered, in a state of agitation. She looked at Tim, then at me. She knew perfectly well why we had convened in that room. "OK. So what can we do?" she said.

I said that if her family wanted to stay in Canada, we could perhaps contact a social worker and find a lawyer. Alicia sighed: "Yeah, but my mom wants us to leave. She has her boyfriend in Jamaica now, and she said they have to do some work on the house." Alicia was so angry, she continued, because she and her sister did not want to leave Canada. "Do you think I could stay here alone with my sister?" she asked.

They were both minors, I said; they had to be with their mother. I felt lacking in words to soothe her or in power to stop her deportation. To clarify our thoughts in that moment of frustration, I asked, "Why would you like to stay here?"

Alicia looked at me and said firmly, "*Everything*, you know? Here, you have more things; you can take the underground or a bus, and you can go everywhere. And *I am used to here*. I have my boyfriend. I have my very good friend Jasna. She is from Slovenia. I don't get along with Canadians; they are too cold. But I call Jasna, and I say, 'What are you up to?' And we plan things together. In Jamaica, I don't have a friend like that—someone I can call when I have things to tell." *I am used to here*. Alicia aligned herself with an array of new habits, which had been unfamiliar before. She had gotten used to here. Importantly, she did so by establishing a network of everyday relationships. She had seen her boyfriend Luke every day for a year. And she had Jasna, her best friend and confidante. It was impossible to separate her everyday habits, her *being here*, from the people she loved.

During our meeting that day, Alicia asked Tim in a pitiful voice, "You think I should go to school?"

Tim kept silent for a while, then asked her back, "What do you think?"

Alicia sunk into her chair and shrugged her shoulders. She looked so powerless, if only for a moment: "Why should I bother to go to school for a few months if I have to go back there *anyways*, where everything is different?"

"Because you learn? Because you have something to do?"

Alicia remained silent. She seemed to understand both Tim's concern and the impossibility of avoiding her family's deportation. Her eyes became wet with tears. "What should I do today?" she asked. Tim said she could help him prepare a theater performance for the following week. Alicia nodded.

As we later walked through a park, Alicia shared with me her fears about her imminent return. She said she would not feel safe in Jamaica: she was afraid that men would physically and verbally harass her on the street. Jamaica was an unsafe and unfamiliar country. She did not have any close friends there, she said. "But here, I have Jasna." She kept silent and added, "My best friend says she will miss me. And I will miss her too. It will be hard without her. We can still call each other, but it won't be the same."

The separation from her boyfriend was also challenging: "It was so difficult to tell him I had to go back. I could not look him in the eyes." A few days later, she decided to send him a text telling him that she wanted to end the relationship altogether. "Why did you break up?" I asked. "I am angry at him," she told me. "He is very possessive and unsure about himself. He is always jealous that I am with other guys. No more of this!" She hesitated for a moment, then quietly said, "Before it was harder to leave, you know, because I had a boyfriend. Now it's easier." Perhaps it is in this hesitation that we need to recognize Alicia's agency. Her reasons for breaking up with Luke included his possessiveness and jealousy. But she also chose to end their relationship instead of facing the pain of a forced separation. She transformed the pain of return into an active feeling: *I am angry at him.*

A month before her deportation, I met Alicia again, at the entrance of the community center. She sat on the stairs with her sister, holding a puppy in her arms. She smiled and told me that this was their new dog. They had named her Puppy. "I don't care so much anymore that I won't go to school for another month," she said. She had lost her cell phone, so she could not text me, she quickly added. As we said goodbye and hugged each other, I knew I would not hear from her again. As I walked away, I heard Alicia and her sister's high-pitched voices: "Puppy! Oooh, Puppyyy!"

## Undocumented Status and Belonging

This fragment of Alicia's story shows what it means, for many young people, to live and to establish relationships in the shadow of deportability. Undocumented status does not only imply the fear of being returned to an unfamiliar country, where one may be exposed to a high degree of violence.[1] Importantly, it also involves the risk of being separated from the affective relationships one has established over the years. The risk of losing the life one has *got used to here*—a life deeply joined with people one loves and cares for.

Like many other young people I met, Alicia described her life in Canada with ambivalence, as a gradual and revocable process of adaptation to *here*—a physical and symbolic place that was anchored to everyday relationships, both powerful and fragile.[2] The importance of these relationships is attested by the fact that, as soon as she knew she would be deported, Alicia estranged herself from her friends and peers. In the act of anticipating loss, she tried to mitigate its enormity.

In the first three chapters of this book, I examined how silent laws and ambiguous practices render young people invisible at a social and political level, partially excluding them from education. In the remaining three chapters, I turn to the effects of undocumented status on young people's lives. In this chapter, I focus on its impacts on social belonging. How do young people navigate everyday relationships when they might be separated from their friends at any moment? And what if they hide themselves and their legal status—in other words, when they conceal a significant part of their daily struggles? What does it mean to belong in spaces of deportability, where feelings of home are so fragile and ill-fitting?

I will reflect on these questions through the voices of Roberto, a boy from Mexico, and Julia, a girl from Jamaica. While scholars have often highlighted how migrants are transformed into subjects who have nowhere to belong,[3] young people's narratives reveal ambiguous experiences of both membership and exclusion. They invite us to understand horizontal forms of recognition that are intrinsic to social relationships and that are *acted* rather than unilaterally imposed. In what follows, we will see how Roberto and Julia come to occupy an ambivalent space of belonging, navigating spaces of both invisibility and recognition—ways of getting used to here, longing and belonging.

## Between Here and There

For many young people, migration drew a line between the new social world they built in Canada and their family life. Roberto migrated from Mexico at the age of eleven with his parents and his older brother. When he first arrived in Montreal, it was difficult to start a new life. He did not understand French and spent a lot of time with his Mexican peers. Every week he went with his parents to a church attended by many undocumented Latin American immigrants. As the months passed, he met friends from other countries and learned to speak French. He gradually developed a social network outside his family and the Mexican community. Like many other young people, he did not keep in contact, or only did so sporadically, with relatives in his country of origin. The memory of his grandmother and his uncles started to fade.

Julia, an eighteen-year-old girl from Jamaica, also told me how the process of adaptation had been easier for her than for her mother:

> She couldn't learn to speak the language because she had to work. My mom had to work to help me and my brother because we were too young to give money. She sacrificed for us. . . . For the parents, it's much more difficult. It is sad that you arrive here with a degree. My mom has a degree in pedagogy, and she ended up working in a factory. It's really difficult. You leave everything; you start from scratch, even though in your country you had a certain status. And here, you're at the bottom. You have to learn new languages; it's difficult for parents.

Julia migrated at age twelve with her mother and younger sister. While Julia was slowly able to create a new life of relationships in Canada, her mother remained socially marginalized:

> My mom doesn't know many people. Besides church, she doesn't have much. She is not like me. I have lots of friends, I am involved in school activities, I have my network, I know lots of people. When I walk on the street, it's sure that I'll meet at least one person that I know! But it's not like that for my mother. When I started to go to school, I started to become involved and to meet people my age. I really started to learn French. They [the school] try, a little bit, to put you in a box (*encadrer*) in the life of Canadian society.

What most helped Julia break out of her family's seclusion were school and the relationships she established with her peers. School, she said, "puts you in a box in the life of Canadian society." This new social environment, with its new habits and norms, inevitably distanced her from the environment of her mother, who mostly relied on a community formed of undocumented migrants from her country of origin.[4]

The affects that young people established, however, were always uncertain and haunted by the possibility of deportation. In one of our conversations, Roberto reflected on the challenges of being split between two realities:[5]

ROBERTO I said to myself, why should I have Mexican friends, since I am here in Canada? I would like to meet people from other countries and to learn French! Then I decided to try a little bit, and now I don't have any Mexican friends anymore. I speak only with Quebecois and people from other countries. And all Mexicans are gone anyways, and I am all alone now.

FRANCESCA They went back to Mexico?

ROBERTO (*Brief silence.*) Yes. (*Silence.*) I lost my Mexican friends, and I have to start another phase of my life again. So it's going to be really hard.

Roberto was caught between two worlds. There were his Mexican friends and the church that his family attended. This was a world of departure and uncertainty, where loss was an everyday issue, or at least always a potentiality. As Roberto said quietly, sadly, "All the Mexicans are gone anyways, and I am all alone now." Perhaps this *anyways* denotes a fracture that occurred and could happen to him at any moment, despite his wishes. At the same time, it also demonstrates the need to resume his own life after this interruption. There was, anyway, yet another world that he had created here, of intimate bonds with people he loved and who did not belong to the Mexican community. This environment was secured by daily activities and physical places around his neighborhood. He played on a football team three times a week—the thing he loved the most about his life in Montreal. He often went to the park with his friends, and his Quebecois girlfriend lived just a ten-minute walk from his apartment. He felt like he belonged here, and yet this feeling was constantly undermined due to his family's deportability.

In his book *The Suffering of the Immigrant*, sociologist Abdelmalek Sayad describes the paradoxical and contradictory condition that migrants experience as a "double absence." For one, they are absent from the community of origin—estranged in social, cultural, and psychological terms. But they are also absent in the society where they build a new life—their residency status is temporary, their citizenship conditional.[6] In his writings, Sayad uses recurring words such as *paradox*, *ambiguity*, and *contradiction* to define the condition of people divided between Algeria and France.[7] In similar ways, undocumented young people in Montreal experience a double absence. They are estranged from both their societies of origin and the Canadian environment. This double absence is also a presence, though partial and conditional. Their entitlement to fully belong is doubly negated by the absence of full membership and, with it, by the impossibility of guaranteeing relationships and a sense of the future.

## Not Disclosing Who You Are

Contradictory feelings of inclusion and exclusion, visibility and invisibility characterized young people's lives. In our conversations and interviews, many young people said that they did not disclose their status to most of their peers and friends. For instance, Roberto said he could not openly reveal his situation to his friends at school and was afraid that they would make fun of him:

ROBERTO When I feel sad, I don't speak of this with my friends. I take my time. I don't have to talk of this because I am afraid.

FRANCESCA What are you afraid of?

ROBERTO That they will say that I have to leave and that they will say that it would be good if I left. Things like that. I'm afraid they are going to laugh at me. That they're not going to understand my situation.

Roberto feared that they would not recognize him as a member of their community. His everyday presence at school was always haunted by an absence—his own deportability and his fear of being misrecognized by others. Julia similarly recounted how she felt invisible to the school bureaucracy. "They just don't know what a refugee claimant is!" she exclaimed once, resentfully. As an example, the school administration charged her for health insurance, which was supposed to be covered by the provincial government. However, this feeling of exclusion was produced not only by the attitude of the school administration but also because she responded by deliberately concealing her legal status. She said, "The teachers don't know; many of my friends don't know. Nobody except for a few people in my close circle knows. It is not something that you're going to tell! My friends and schools wouldn't understand why I can't travel like them, why I pay nonresident tuition fees." She and her family often felt isolated: "Around us, everyone was either already gone or already with all the papers. So we have been, like, in a juridical void for a long time. You're stuck there. You don't move, you do nothing, you can't do anything." Her friends, she said, perhaps sensed something, but they didn't know her exact circumstances: "I didn't tell them all my story. Even my close friends—they know I have to pay more fees and that I need to work, but they don't know more than that. But they helped me in some ways—if I need money, for instance—though they don't really know about my status."

The perception of herself as undocumented was shaped by a paradox. In her daily life, Julia was invisible—her existence ignored by the bureaucratic state and her peers. In response, she masked her identity and didn't disclose a significant part of who she was. Like Roberto, she anticipated other people wouldn't understand her predicament.

## Making Sense of Place

While concealing their daily struggles, young people carved out spaces of belonging and established significant relationships with peers. The significance of these bonds was acutely felt when young people were deported.[8] Roberto, for instance, was heartbroken to leave his Quebecois girlfriend: "I'm so sad to leave her, especially because it's two years now that we've been together. It's sooo sad. It's too bad." Two months before being deported, he reiterated his desire to stay in Canada: "We came here, and it was too hard for me. It was a new phase of my life, and I was sad I was leaving my country. But now I am happy to be here in Canada, and the only thing I don't want is to go back to my country because I'm used to here, with my friends and my girlfriend, and I don't really want to leave. I want to stay here." *I am used to here. I am happy to be here. I want to stay here.* There is a stubborn repetition in these words. A desire for emplacement that Roberto firmly repeated: *here, here, here.* Though it was initially very difficult to leave Mexico and adapt to his new life, he said he now felt happy in Canada. So happy that the only thing he didn't want was to return to Mexico. His sense of "here" grew together with the relationships he created—with his friends, with his girlfriend. Most importantly, Roberto mobilized his process of adaptation to a place as a claim of belonging. He framed his right to remain and resist his family's deportation by the fact that he had gotten used to here. "I don't want to come back to my country *because* I'm used to here, with my friends and my girlfriend," he said.

Roberto's words do not define a clear and discursive statement of possession. Rather, they entail a gradual and shifting sense of adaptation to and acceptance of a physical and emotional space. A continuous process of being and longing for a place, a *here*. To be sure, place is constituted not only by a physical setting but by the meanings attached to it.[9] Keith Basso, in his ethnography *Wisdom Sits in Places*, provides a powerful account of the meanings that animate an environment. A sense of place, Basso argues, is an idea of home: "Local landscapes where groups of men and women have invested themselves (their thoughts, their values, their collective sensibilities) and to which they feel they belong."[10] In more pressing or subtle ways, we inevitably become attached to a place: "It is then we come to see that attachments to places may be nothing less than profound and that when these attachments are threatened, we feel in jeopardy too."[11]

The sentence "I am used to here" points to the revocable and precarious ways young people occupied and claimed everyday spaces. Young people came to profoundly relate to unfamiliar landscapes. But there was not enough time, not enough security to fully attach themselves to where they lived. Instead, they could only get used to here. It couldn't be otherwise, as their *here* was haunted by the possibility of being dislocated again. Roberto's belonging moved between movements of emplacement and displacement; it pointed to a slow adaptation to his family's decision to migrate and his desire to re-create new communities here.[12]

Yet in defining their belonging as an ambiguous process of adaptation, young people could not escape their relationships of dependence to their families and the community of undocumented migrants. Julia made this clear to me when I asked her if she felt at home here (*Est-ce que tu te sens un peu comme chez toi ici?*): "I am not in an environment where there are many immigrants because almost all my friends are Quebecois. So I have become used to here. But I see the other side with my mother: her social environment is made up only of immigrants. Sometimes she is depressed because she cannot get used to here. She always meets people whose migratory status is fuzzy and uncertain. So she cannot escape from this kind of social group. She cannot escape from exclusion because she is always with people who are excluded." Again, *I have become used to here*: a precarious, conditional process. But also, most importantly, her words defied my question. Instead of directly addressing the issue of belonging, Julia used communicative strategies that hinged on ambiguity. She made space for her contrasting identities to coexist. Even if she could get used to here, unlike her mother, she could not see herself completely apart from her family. Nor could she imagine herself as entirely part of her Quebecois peers' environment. In this sense, by representing herself as undocumented, Julia voiced the concerns of a community of excluded people to which she was intimately related. And she defied, in important ways, essentialized notions of what being undocumented as well as belonging to someone and to somewhere might mean.

## On Belonging

Young people's narratives reveal a sense of belonging that is both powerful and fleeting, ebbing and flowing. How can we understand these precarious movements? What can they teach us about membership? To answer these questions, we first need to clarify what we mean by belonging—a notion that is often taken for granted, left undefined, or vaguely assimilated to ideas of identity and citizenship.[13] In the *Oxford English Dictionary*, the word *belonging* has two sets of meaning. First, there is a vertical denotation: to be the property of, to be due to, and even to be dominated by. Second, there is a horizontal connotation: to have an affinity for a place or situation, to have the personal and social attributes to be a member of a group. This suggests that belonging has two interlocked faces: the ways we belong depend on how we are recognized as members of a community.

Theorizations on belonging put this relationship at their centers. An example is the work of the sociologist Nira Yuval-Davis, who has offered one of the most comprehensive analyses on the subject. In *The Politics of Belonging*, she differentiates between a vertical dimension (which she terms "the politics of belonging") and a horizontal one (which she defines as "belonging"). The *politics* of belonging includes political projects that draw boundaries of membership between who is entitled to belong and who is not. The emotional counterpart of this politics, Yuval-Davis suggests, is what defines *belonging*. Depending on whether policies include or reject us, she argues, we may feel positive or negative emotions. This insight helps us understand the source of young people's frustration. The young people I encountered felt pain, anger, and fear because they could not identify themselves as part of the community of citizens.[14] These negative feelings were typically tied to negative experiences of membership. To put it simply, our sense of belonging is impaired when we are excluded.

Yuval-Davis defines a positive sense of belonging as "feeling 'at home,' feeling 'safe,' and if not necessarily feeling in control, at least feeling able enough generally to predict expectations and rules of behavior."[15] Yet this definition doesn't allow us to fully understand the complex psychological dimensions of young people—their mixed feelings of exclusion and inclusion or the paradoxes of their condition. To be sure, young people don't feel safe. But sometimes they might feel at home, anchored to a sense of here, on a good day when undocumented status does not cast its shadow. They don't feel they have control over the government's deportation order, yet they can resist the constraints on their lives in subtle ways.

## Nowhere to Belong?

Yuval-Davis, like many other scholars, grounds her theorization in a binary correlation between recognition and belonging that oscillates from positive to negative.[16] Such theorizations expect that we form a positive sense of belonging when we are recognized as entitled citizens. But if the state doesn't recognize us, it is often implied that we wouldn't be able to develop a sense of attachment—feeling at home, safe, and in control.[17] Charles Taylor, for instance, suggests that without an orienting framework of full belonging and recognition, "we would be unable to derive meaning from our lives—we would not know 'who we are' and where we are coming from."[18] Misrecognition would then cause us harm and oppression; we would find ourselves at sea.

Scholars who have analyzed the experiences of undocumented young people have frequently drawn on similar assumptions. Often, they have emphasized how restrictive immigration policies have detrimental effects on people's sense of belonging[19] and how undocumented status plays as an additional factor of instability.[20] It renders children betwixt and between, with nowhere to belong.[21] This in-between condition has been particularly examined in relation to the transition into adulthood of 1.5-generation undocumented youth in the United States—that is, children who migrate to a new country before or during their early teens. Writing about this group, Roberto Gonzales argues that undocumented young people are able to gain a secure sense of belonging as American citizens when they have full access to education and their parents' support.[22] However, when they enter adulthood and they are asked for the documents they lack, young people "awaken to a nightmare." The lack of documents becomes their primary status, and they find themselves with no place to belong.[23]

These examinations, as important as they are in showing the exclusionary nature of the politics of belonging, remain inadequate to describe its psychological component. They fail to describe how undocumented status is not unilaterally imposed but navigated and suffused in affective relationships. They don't do justice, for instance, to the ways Alicia coped with her imminent deportation—her apparently contradictory feelings of sadness, anger, and happiness. While she could not look her boyfriend in the eyes and face the enormity of his pain (her pain), she also felt angry at him and decided to end their relationship. And while she deeply suffered the separation from the people she loved, she bought a new puppy, which she cheerfully held on her lap.

It might be tempting to say that young people have nowhere to belong. To be sure, it is a claim that can serve to advocate that certain groups of people *should* be entitled to be part of the community of citizens. In a time of growing xenophobia and racist policies, this is a pressing political demand. I partake in the urgency of this claim. When we see the tangible and deadly effects of injustice, our discourses inevitably become moral ones about inclusion and rights to citizenship. And yet we must be careful not to correlate too hastily our political claims with people's psychic lives.

The problem with these theorizations, I argue, is that they sustain an idea of belonging that is mostly defined from a normative and deficit perspective. Implicitly or explicitly, these frameworks revolve around the immigrants' adaptation to and integration in what is defined the "host country." They imply a linear trajectory—one where we know where we come from, who we are, and where we are going. They keep posing the question of whether or not young people belong and, most importantly, whether they will ever belong. And the answer often given to this question of belonging is no, these young people have nowhere to belong.

The primary attribute defining the condition of young people then becomes *lack*: the deprivation of identity, the failure to become incorporated, a condition of being stuck in a liminal phase where they wait to become complete.[24] Young people are considered not one or another—strange creatures, neither fish nor fowl. But to portray young people in these privative terms describes nothing, if only the act of not being one thing or another. An ontology of lacking doesn't help us understand ways of being here and there or of getting used to here—however partial these forms of presence might be, they are *presence* nonetheless.

The question, then, is not whether young people belong or do not belong, or if they will one day belong. Rather, it is how we can understand ambivalent ways of belonging as conditions in their own right. We need to detach ourselves from normative views suggesting that the solution to the conundrum is full "integration" in the terms that society expects migrants to assimilate. We need to sweep away this tangible pessimism about the possibility of having multiple and ambiguous belongings and still carrying on with life. These pessimistic perspectives reproduce binary principles of either-or, in-out, and us-them without capturing the connections between symbolic and social spaces that run deep in young people's lives.

## In Between

What I suggest here is to examine how *either* and *or*, *in* and *out*, and *us* and *them* might coexist conflictingly and simultaneously in the lives of young people. I argue that ambivalence—the coexistence of conflicting feelings, enduring tensions, and insoluble contradictions—deeply permeates young people's narratives.[25] It shapes their ways of being with spatial and temporal fractures, with movements of emplacement and displacement—here and there. Young people belong in between, in spaces where they can only get used to being.

Psychoanalytic theory has long argued that all affective relationships involve a certain degree of ambivalence.[26] When we enter a relationship, we are called into being through identifying ourselves to the other. This process of identification foregrounds our very desire to exist but is also fraught with ambivalence, as full identification is never possible. In the case of socially marginalized groups such as undocumented young people, however, the desire to exist is constantly fraught with tension.

To understand how these tensions are reproduced for undocumented young people, I find helpful the reflections of Homi Bhabha, who has drawn on psychoanalytical theory to examine postcolonial contexts. Bhabha suggests that colonial relationships are *primarily* characterized as spaces of splitting and ambivalence.[27] For the colonized subject, Bhabha argues, the close link between the "self" and the "other" always leads to uncertainty and disillusionment because it is always defined in terms of difference. The colonial discourse, he tells us, is like a snake in the grass, which speaks "in a tongue that is forked."[28] It recognizes the "other" through a contradictory process that oscillates "from mimicry—a difference that is almost nothing but not quite—to menace—a difference that is almost total but not quite."[29] It is this slippage—a difference that is almost the same *but not quite*—that produces ambivalence. Trapped by a forked tongue, the subject is caught in uncertainty. A partial presence, always incomplete. Undocumented young people are similarly trapped in ambivalent relationships: contradictory instances of camouflage and subtle resistance, misrecognition and identification.

I am not alone in arguing for the need to add nuance to and complexify notions of belonging. I find good company in feminist critiques that conceive of belonging as a dynamic process of place-making, dialectically determined by both the state and its subjects.[30] These critiques have challenged rigid notions of belonging as an ontologically solid state of being. Other scholars have also explored how undocumented young people are situated across different spaces.[31] Patricia Zavella, in her ethnography *I'm Neither Here nor There*, illuminates the unstable position of Mexican migrants who have their "eyes on both sides of the border."[32] Their transnational identity, she argues, "includes feelings that one is neither from here nor from there, nor at home anywhere."[33]

The work of Gloria Anzaldúa, feminist scholar and poet, is also relevant here. In her book *Borderlands / La Frontera*, she ponders what it means to live at the borderland as a *mestiza*, growing up between Mexican and Anglo-American cultures: "Living on borders and in margins, keeping intact one's shifting and multiple identity and integrity, is like trying to swim in a new element, an 'alien' element. . . . And yes, the 'alien' element has become familiar—never comfortable, not with society's clamor to uphold the old, to rejoin the flock, to go with the herd. No, not comfortable but home."[34] Her reflection is an invitation to listen for ambiguity, to understand dangerous and uncomfortable feelings of home.[35] In these spaces, she argues, people become split: "The coming together of opposite qualities within."[36] She says, "Today we ask to be met halfway."[37] To meet people halfway is not just a theoretical statement. It is an invitation and a provocation, pointing to the materiality of ambivalence in the lives of young people.

## Ambivalent Belongings

In this chapter, I have examined the struggles of young people floating in an uncertain state, caught between the desire to belong and the impossibility of fully belonging—here and not here. *I have become used to here*, young people repeat. These words point to an ambivalent, conditional process of longing for and belonging to a place. But most importantly, they defy categorical questions: to belong or not belong, to feel at home or not. These are not the right questions. In their narratives, young people avoided certain words (home, belonging) that were perhaps troubling, were too confining, or simply did not reflect their realities. Instead of portraying themselves as not fully belonging, they circumvented the thorny issue altogether. They framed themselves as getting used to a precise physical and symbolic place—*here*. They made space for contrasting desires and identities to coexist.

Ambivalence deeply shaped the affective relationships of young people. I suggest two reasons for this ambivalence. First, young people could not fully belong because the state (through immigration policies, teachers, school administration) failed to recognize them. Second, young people responded to this misrecognition by deliberately masking their identities and by ambivalently positioning themselves in relation to others. They performed the gesture of hiding their status from their teachers, their classmates, and even their closest friends. To the people they loved, they camouflaged their identities, acting as if they were *almost the same*. There was always the possibility that their friends would turn their backs and say, "You're not one of us; we don't love you anymore."

In a context where being seen comes with the possibility of rejection, ambivalence protected young people from the risks of a wounded attachment. It was a tactic to distance themselves from those who didn't recognize them, to be shielded from the pain of being separated from the ones they loved. By occupying—ambivalently—affective spaces in between, young people detached themselves from the disempowering conditions they were caught in. These narratives teach us that to belong is always an ambivalent matter of interdependence. The ways young people established affective relationships across different communities were always ill-fitting. They could not anchor them entirely—only halfway. And it is by going halfway that we will be able to finally meet young people.

# 5

## Double Binds

After she had left her family and her home country, Colombia, at age twelve, Elizabeth had started a long journey on the run. She had crossed Central America and Mexico before arriving in the United States and then migrated to Canada six years later. At the U.S.-Mexico border, the patrol had pursued her with dogs in the dark. She ran until she was caught. She was sent on a plane to a youth detention center in Texas, where she was held for one year.

Every night during the ten years she was without legal status, Elizabeth dreamed about that long run at the U.S.-Mexico border. "In my dreams, I always *ran, ran, ran* from Immigration. I was naked, cold, and vulnerable," she recounted. As she ran through the streets, she heard immigration officers shooting at her back, their dogs barking in the distance. She frantically tried to hide in the bushes and in the woods. Yet night after night, she was found and arrested. Every single night the same nightmare, the same ending.

Elizabeth remembered how pain entered her nights: "I had many traumas. The trauma of living with the violence in my family but also the new trauma of escaping and crossing so many countries—and the trauma of being followed by Immigration in the U.S. So that is a lot that can add more trauma and more trauma. This is the reason why I had those nightmares, because of all the trauma I had." In her dreams she reenacted "all those emotions, all those dark sides of what it is like being illegal. What is it to have fear, to hide, to feel alone and isolated about everything." "In those years [living without legal status in the U.S.], I started to leave home and be homeless. I had nowhere to stay. I felt isolated, alone, cold, naked on the streets. I had nowhere to go," she told me.

I asked her if, in those years, there were any places where she felt somewhat safe. She looked me in the eyes and said, "I never felt safe." "Never," I murmured. She repeated firmly, "I *never* felt safe," and continued,

> Every time I ran, every time I hid, I was afraid of either dying of hunger—because I had to run in the desert in Texas—or being killed by the Mexican police, or being killed by many policemen in the United States, or being killed by Immigration, or being killed by anybody because of being illegal in these countries. By being illegal, you are a target, so you are easily hurt. Anything can happen to you when you are not allowed to live in a country and you do not have ID. You do not have the same rights as everybody else, so you live a life where you do not feel like you are in charge of your life. So you feel obliged to hide or to run because that is the way it is.

For a long time, there were no places to be safe and call home. Nowhere to stay, only places to run from. Her life continuously shifted between hiding and being on the run. *Hiding*: forced to live in spaces where she felt she didn't exist, in corners where invisibility temporarily protected her. *Running*: exposed to vulnerability, fleeing for her own survival—again.

In this chapter, we will follow Elizabeth's story to understand how undocumented status shaped her psychic life with double binds—paradoxical situations where she was trapped between the movements of hiding and running, of being invisible and on the spot. Through a journey between Elizabeth's narrative and artwork, we will examine how she turned these double binds into a space in which new ways of imagining life emerged.

## The Dark Sides of Being Undocumented

The "dark sides of being illegal" are what Elizabeth calls the physical and psychological conditions of being unsafe: so profound that they entered her body and her dreams. These dark sides evoke what Sarah Willen has described as the "embodied, experiential consequence" of living without status.[1] Undocumented status becomes a bodily condition of "abject life,"[2] an existence subject to exploitation.[3] In Elizabeth's story, it means to be exposed to injury in her life, to run naked in her dreams. The danger of death is repeated in her narrative again and again. She could die during the perilous border crossing. She could be killed by U.S. or Mexican border patrol. She could be murdered by anybody.[4]

This hazard of injury is deeply connected to the murderous potential of the state—the hidden truth that governments can expose certain people to death.[5] Foucault reminds us that modern nations have the power to make certain people live and let others die.[6] Racism, he argues, is "a way of introducing a break into the domain of life that is under power's control: the break between what must live and what must die."[7] The ways the state controls the lives of *us* citizens go hand in hand with the ways it lets die others who are labeled as *them, illegal.*[8]

It is important to remember that the risk of death does not necessarily involve physical murder. More often, it is embedded in forms of "social death"—the condition of extreme loss and social disenfranchisement experienced by groups of people who are highly marginalized and not recognized as fully human.[9] Achille Mbembe argues that in colonial contexts, this space in between life and death is often used as the main technique of governing. The slave, he writes, "is kept alive but in a state of injury. Slave life, in many ways, is a form of death-in-life."[10] Giorgio Agamben has also theorized about these precarious forms of life caught in the risk of harm.[11] He suggests that the paradigm of modern politics is constituted by the figure of *homo sacer*. Represented by refugees and groups who are outcasts from the political community, the *homo sacer* is a bare life deemed not worth living. A naked body that can be killed without notice, without sound, in a perilous border crossing.

This condition of vulnerability poignantly emerges in Elizabeth's nightmares through her act of running naked from immigration officers without the possibility of escape. In her story *The Ones Who Walk Away from Omelas*, Ursula Le Guin tells of a child confined in a city.[12] Here's the story. Omelas is a happy town that bursts with the sweetness of a fairy tale, and music winds through its green meadows. Its citizens are "mature, intelligent, passionate adults whose lives were not wretched."[13] They are content people, with the comforts of technology and all the wonderful devices that make life easier. They do not use swords, nor do they keep slaves or have a king. They don't need them, as evil and violence seem not to exist.

But as we can already anticipate, there is always a shadow in the insistent presence of life, something buried in the overt celebration of happiness. Under the buildings of Omelas, there is a room, a dark and filthy cellar. Inside, there is a child. We cannot say if they are a boy or a girl or how old they are. We know that the child can still remember the sunlight and her mother's voice but not how long she has been in the cellar. Time has no dimension here. She is thin, her body infested with sores. She is naked.

At times, someone comes to kick her or just to look at her with disgust. The child says, "I will be good. Please let me out. I will be good!" Nobody replies. She speaks less and less often and finally only emits indecipherable sounds. She cannot be cleaned, fed, or comforted, let alone released. For if these things are done, all the happiness and prosperity of the town will vanish. Only when the young citizens of Omelas reach the age of twelve is the child shown to them—a macabre initiation into adulthood, an admonition about the terms of their happiness.

The story of Omelas brings us closer to understanding how Elizabeth can dream every night of running naked through the streets. At the other end of the spectrum of life for citizens is a naked child who, like Elizabeth, can be left to die. The lack of documents confines her to hidden niches of society: an underground labor economy, a life on the run, a community exposed to injury. In Omelas, the prosperity of a city depends on a child's exclusion and suffering. Elizabeth's story is even bleaker: her suffering is forgotten, her life exposed to an anonymous death. Through her rejection, the nation-state keeps to its citizens the promise of securing borders. The order of the state depends on her confinement in invisibility.

## Running as a Child

The fact that, under the luxurious palaces of Omelas, there is a naked *child* is revealing. Her vulnerability is linked not only to the murderous nature of the state but also to her status as a minor. In important ways, Elizabeth can become a target because she is undocumented *and* a child.[14] The impossibility of returning to her home country, the violence she experienced at a young age, and the lack of family support exacerbated her uncertainty and suffering. In Arizona, where she lived for six years, she worked in a factory. She entered a life of undocumented labor and exploitation that was shared by many adults. She explained, "I worked there under the table because I was a minor. I was a kid, and I did not have money. The only way I could survive was by working. There was no way for me to become legal, so for me it was difficult to live like everybody else living there." She told me, "I did not have any choice, and I did not have my chance." This loss of control over her life was caused by a double vulnerability: her undocumented status and her young age.

As we have seen in chapter 1, undocumented children hold an ambiguous and contradictory position as minors in need of protection *and* undocumented migrants to be rejected. Immigration authorities resolve the intractability of this status by considering young people's presence as predominantly based on their lack of documents rather than their need for protection as minors. This is exemplified by Elizabeth's account of her asylum application while she was waiting in a youth detention center in Texas. In the asylum claim, she found it difficult to assemble, in a coherent way, all the unspeakable experiences that she had faced. She had escaped from family violence in her home country, she had survived dangerous border crossings, and she was caught after running for hours and hours. She said, "It was hard for me to explain everything because it was not easy for me to remember and to give all the specific dates the immigration officer wanted. You do not have documents, and you cannot remember everything because it is just too much trauma. I was confused, and at the same time, it was very hard for me to talk about all that trauma."

The immigration officer who judged her claim considered Elizabeth's story to lack credibility. She spent many hours to establish whether the case was, as Elizabeth put it, "true or fake." Elizabeth said that the officer was "very hard" and did not understand "all the stories and violence that [she] faced." But most importantly, the validity of her story was discredited by her status as a minor. As Elizabeth said, "It was not believable that, at twelve years old, I could have done what I did." Her agency—that is, her capacity to flee her home country and embark on a journey alone—was negated by the fact she was a child. The officer merely considered her "illegal" in the national territory and urged her to leave the country. Elizabeth said, "She judged me by how many visas it took me to cross many countries. And I literally crossed many countries, and I abused many laws by crossing one country to another." She remembered the harsh words of the officer: "You must leave, and I will make sure that you leave. This is not only you. Every other kid has to leave because there is a law, and the government does not want just anybody to be in this country."

As an undocumented child, Elizabeth embodied two conflicting realities: she was both a vulnerable child in need of protection and one who was capable of crossing borders. The immigration officer was unable to consider that forms of vulnerability and agency might simultaneously cohabit in one subject. She negated Elizabeth's vulnerability as a minor *because* of her undocumented status. Elizabeth was not recognized for who she said she was: a child who had lost the intelligibility of her life and yet had the ability to face the difficulties of the journey alone.

## The Deadly Space Between

The failure to understand Elizabeth's narrative relates not only to immigration decisions but also, more broadly, to our ambivalence toward young people. We often struggle to recognize the coexistence of vulnerability and agency in children's lives, as we often fail to do so in our own lives. We tend to flatten contradictions when we evaluate and judge human actions.

I would like to examine here the ambiguity represented by Elizabeth's status and how, ultimately, the law tried to resolve it. In thinking about these issues, I find company in the reflections of Barbara Johnson, particularly in her analysis of Herman Melville's novel *Billy Budd*.[15] In this story, we meet three oddly assorted characters.[16] Billy Budd, an innocent and good-looking sailor with a stutter; John Claggart, a ship's master-at-arms who seems to possess a natural depravity; and Captain Vere, a bookish commanding officer. Claggart unjustly charges Billy Budd with conspiring to mutiny. Against this accusation, Billy Budd stutters and is unable to defend himself. In a narrative twist, he becomes enraged and kills his accuser. Captain Vere ultimately condemns him to hang.

What intrigues Johnson about this story is the opacity of the two main characters: the innocent one kills, and the evil one dies. When he describes the two, Melville admits his hesitation. A straightforward depiction would be insufficient to fathom Claggart's mystery. "For the adequate comprehending of Claggart by a normal nature, these hints are insufficient. To pass from a normal nature to him one must cross *the deadly space between*. And this is best done by indirection," Melville writes (emphasis mine).[17] In reading this passage, Johnson pauses, and we pause with her. How can we define this deadly space between? she ponders. "The expression 'deadly space between' primarily points to a gap in cognition, a boundary beyond which understanding does not normally go. This sort of space, as a limit to comprehension, seems to be an inherent attempt to describe Claggart," Johnson explains.[18] It is a description that doesn't hit its object, pointing to a gap between sign and referent, object and meaning. It is a space that can even be deadly, where an innocent-looking sailor kills, and a wicked man dies as the victim.

Johnson suggests that the primary function, as well as the violence, of judgment is "to convert an ambiguous situation into a decidable one." Law then creates bounded categories to make the deadly space *less* between. Captain Vere is called to judge Billy Budd's murderous act and to resolve his ambiguity—his sudden shift from victim to assassin. What helps Vere solve the puzzle is the rigor of the law. If he had delved into the opacity of Billy Budd's conscience, he would have found it impossible to make a clear judgment.

The law helps us translate the ambiguity of the difference *within* one subject—in which two conflicting entities problematize the very idea of an entity—into a predictable difference *between* subjects, in which two opposing forces presuppose that all things are definite and knowable. In the case of Elizabeth, the judge resolved the coexistence of agency and vulnerability, the ambiguities of her story, into a polarized difference—her vulnerable status as a child and her undocumented status. The law draws a definite line. It annihilates internal contradictions and establishes its authority in an interpretative violence.[19] It is a way of dealing with the deadly space between by eradicating its mystery.

Elizabeth's paradoxical position—as a vulnerable *and* an agentive child—can be described as a deadly space between. She is an ambiguous presence, one that is difficult to describe or even to name. The immigration officer could not grant her protection because she was not vulnerable enough, not child enough. Elizabeth unsettled common assumptions about what it means to be a child. She raised troubling questions that had no answer. How could she have embarked on a migration journey at only twelve years of age? How could she have lost the coherence of a life without losing herself?

## As If

In listening to young people's experiences, I often asked myself how I could understand or write about what is ambiguous and not evidently manifest. How could I fathom the complex predicament young people are caught in—being both vulnerable and agentic—or the interplay between their constraints and resistance to those constraints? Melville argues that describing the complexity of human nature is hardly possible. It would mean to "enter its labyrinth and get out again, without a clue derived from some source other than what is known as 'knowledge of the world.'"[20] He continues, "In an average man of the world, his constant rubbing with it blunts that fine spiritual insight indispensable to the understanding of the essential in certain exceptional characters, whether evil ones or good." Then, to understand the heart of an innocent-looking sailor who murders, we need to cross the deadly space between. And this, Melville suggests, "is best done by indirection."[21]

Following Melville's insights, Johnson argues that we can understand indirection as a middle ground between the position of a naive and an ironic reader. The naive reader finds meaning in the surface of things and "takes every sign as transparently readable, as long as what he reads is consistent with transparent peace, order, and authority."[22] The ironic reader, on the other hand, interprets reality to confirm his own doubts and ultimately to prove the absence of meaning and truth. Both readers, Johnson argues, "do violence to the plays of ambiguity and belief by forcing upon the text the applicability of a universal and absolute law."[23]

I would like to attend here to the suggestion of taking a middle path, in the attempt to do justice to the opacity of Elizabeth's story. It would be reductive to interpret her experience merely as a condition of bare life. As we will see later, while undocumented status severely constrained her life, she carried on, negotiated, and imagined life *as if* it were otherwise. With the locution *as if*, I would like to point to the ways she endured uncertainty and found moments of respite in fragments of possibility and intimate connections where life could be imagined otherwise.

We can find a sensitive account of these spaces in the collection of images and texts entitled *After the Last Sky*, by Edward Said and the photographer Jean Mohr.[24] Here, Palestinian lives are portrayed in the obstinacy of everyday life. We see people playing cards under a tree in an open-air café, raising their children, cooking meals for their families, or conversing on a terrace with a lovely view over the city. Said describes these images as an attempt to render the condition of exile "not from the viewpoint of policymakers but that of memoirists and unregimented historians. It is an unreconciled book, in which the contradictions and antinomies of our lives and experiences remain as they are, assembled neither (I hope) into neat wholes nor into sentimental ruminations about the past. Fragments, memories, disjointed scenes, intimate particulars."[25] In similar ways, I would like to attend to Elizabeth's story and listen to the tensions and open-ended spaces that infuse her life.

## The Sea, a Wheat Field

We can better understand these spaces through the photographs that Elizabeth took about her nightmares. The idea of photography occurred to her one day when she was living undocumented in Canada. From the little balcony of her apartment, she pondered what the future held for her. She said, "It was one of those days when I did not know what to do about my future. I did not know anything. But I did not lose hope. I was very hopeful of what might come of the future." She said, "I realized that I had a gift for photos, and I started to take more and more photos that I liked." At the core of her passion, she continued, there was "the need to communicate something." Most importantly, she longed to convey her hardships: "My photos are about when I was alone and had no support. I had nightmares, and in my nightmares, most of the time I was naked and cold with no help. So my photos reflect the moments where I felt isolated, alone, cold, naked on the streets. I need to express those feelings; I need to express those moments in my photos." Since then, she always carries her camera wherever she goes, so naturally that it looks like an integral part of her body.

In a series of black-and-white photographs, Elizabeth represented her nightmares. In these pictures, she transferred her experience to the body of Rodrigo, her best friend for many years. Rodrigo came from Mexico and was also undocumented. A few years after the pictures were taken, he was deported to his home country, and Elizabeth lost contact with him. The few times she told me about him, her eyes became wet with tears.

In the images, Rodrigo is naked, as Elizabeth was in her dreams. He is partially hidden from our gaze; we can only see his back. He bends down with his arms over his head, which has fallen between his knees, as if to protect himself. In one photograph, he lies on the tracks of an abandoned railway. The nudity of his curved back and the sharp line of his spine blends in with the barrenness of the surroundings. In another image, he is crouched in front of a broken window, of which only the skeletal steel frame and a few pieces of glass remain. He holds the bars of the window, looking outside—perhaps at the trees, the cobbled road, or at something else we can't see. In another series of images, we see Rodrigo nude again and enclosed by wide, natural spaces. We find him kneeling, surrounded by the sea. Water swirls around his feet. In another image, he stands again in front of the sea. His arms are outstretched, embracing the horizon. We find him, another time, in the middle of a wheat field. He waves his arms in a joyful gesture toward the sky; the wheat spikes dance in the wind. We can only see his back, but this time, the world opens up in front of him.

## Double Binds

Elizabeth's photographs, refractions of her own nightmares, represent her life as shaped by a latent *vulnerability*—abandoned urban corners, where one is ducked on the ground and friends might be separated. But they also illuminate openings of *potentiality*—a sea, a wheat field, where new possibilities of life still exist. They vacillate between constraints and desires that pose dilemmas and prevent resolution.

How do we consider the ambiguities of these representations? What can they tell us about life without legal status and, more generally, life in marginal spaces? In analyzing how such paradoxes shape subjectivities—how they are generated and negotiated—I find it useful to think through the reflections of Gregory Bateson. Analyzing the communication dynamics of people affected by schizophrenia, Bateson observed that they often find themselves in a "double bind."[26] This happens when an individual receives conflicting messages in a vitally important relationship (i.e., a relationship that is essential for their survival) and struggles to make sense of the experience.[27] Take, for instance, a child who is told two contradictory things by her mother. The child is not able to resolve this contradiction and decide which is the "right" message. She is afraid to ask for clarification because this would mean disappointing her mother. The child then becomes stuck and learns to perceive the world in a double-bind pattern.

To be sure, these double binds happen not only for schizophrenic patients but every time we are put on the spot. Let's imagine, for instance, that we need to respond to a contradictory statement that we don't fully understand. Sometimes, we simply ask the other person to clarify the statement: "What exactly do you mean?" or "What do you really want me to do?" But other times, when we feel we are in a vulnerable position and open opposition carries a risk to our own survival, we can't ask to clarify the message.

In the case of Elizabeth and many other young people I befriended, the production of double binds was central to their existence. It happened through the force and frequency that paradoxical situations generate. Undocumented status then constitutes a condition where individuals constantly feel trapped, simultaneously invisible and put on the spot. In her dreams as in her life, Elizabeth shifted between acts of hiding and running, without any possibility of escape. She hid, as she might easily be harmed or killed. And when the possibility of being injured came closer, she ran but without escaping. The immigration authorities would arrest her night after night.

## Dreams and Images

One winter afternoon, Elizabeth and I were aimlessly hanging out. We entered a photography shop. She wanted to buy a new camera, though she didn't really have the money. While she was contemplating different cameras, she told me, "You know, pictures saved me. They helped me so much all these years I was undocumented."

How did pictures save her? Perhaps Bateson's insights are again helpful to understand. He suggests that when a double bind seems unescapable, metaphors can offer safety.[28] A metaphor, he argues, allows us both to describe reality and to indirectly resist a situation that we perceive as unjust. It provides us with a haven by enabling us to be somewhere else, to become someone else. Elizabeth shifted her suffering to metaphors both through her artwork and in her dreams. The psychiatrist Ludwig Binswanger suggests that the imagistic nature of dreams has a liberating power, even a redemptive function, when we experience pain. He describes the experience of suffering as "falling from the clouds." It is a physical act of tottering, sinking, falling—a bitter sense of uprootedness when our hopes and expectations prove illusory. When pain makes us fall, the pictorial representations of dreams help us keep our feet on the ground. In a dream, Binswanger suggests, "I no longer fall from the clouds as an individual alone in my pain. It is, rather, my pain itself that falls at my feet as a second dramatis persona. This is a most outspoken expression of my ability, under certain circumstances, to 'purely physically' keep my feet on the ground even as I fall and introspectively observe my own falling."[29] In other words, we can see our pain as *other*; we can look at our own falling and still stay standing. As the dreamer awakens, he seeks to "take hold of the dynamics in these events, 'himself'—the moment, that is, when he resolves to bring continuity or consequence into a life that rises and falls, falls and rises. Only then does he *make* something. What he actually makes is the history of his own life, his inner life-history."[30]

In the case of Elizabeth, the reappropriation of suffering takes place at a double level. First, through her nightmares, she interpreted her experience of being undocumented and the trauma she faced. She saw herself running naked through the streets again and again. Second, through photography, she resignified her trauma by shifting it to somewhere else (the ambiguity of pictorial representations) and to someone else (her beloved friend). In her photographs, she represented her vulnerability and, perhaps most importantly, moments of hope and respite. She could see her life not only as an experience of falling but also through moments of rising and opening. Her photographs reveal how double binds can be both anchored and resisted through the imagination of open-ended spaces that could offer her safety—the sea, a wheat field. Her nightmares were transformed, her naked body transported into spaces of possibility. Ultimately, the ambiguity of images allowed her to make sense of the double binds constraining her life yet without entirely resolving them.

## Fallen Angels

Two of Elizabeth's photographs have become part of my imagination. One is of Rodrigo bent down on the railway track, his arms over his head. The other is the one in which he opens his arms before the sea, looking toward the horizon. One morning, as I cycled, these two pictures appeared to me in a sequence. The young man fell on the railway tracks, then he stood up. He embraced the line between the sea and the sky, where there was no end and no beginning but the certainty of a horizon. Or perhaps, I thought, it was the other way around: after Rodrigo turned his gaze away from the sea, the earth faltered beneath his feet.

As I thought about these images, suddenly another fragment of memory emerged. Once, when I was living in the United States, my friend Juan invited me to spend the weekend with his family in the countryside. In the bedroom where I slept, I stumbled onto a painting hanging on the wall. It captured and unsettled me. It was of a dark devil lying down, knees against his chest, in a melancholy pose, which was uncannily similar to Elizabeth's image. "Did you paint this?" I asked. "I did, when I was undocumented and life was so hard," Juan said. He paused for a moment, then added, "This was me, my life. A fallen angel." My friend once told me he had lived for many years without legal status. But I never dared to ask anything. His words were brief and ended in silence. They belonged to a past he did not want to remember.

Fallen angels, in the Abrahamic traditions, are angels who have sinned and have been cast out of heaven to fall onto the earth. As I remembered Juan's self-portrait, in my mind, it overlapped with Elizabeth's depictions of her nightmares. Rodrigo, bent down in an empty urban space, might also be a fallen angel. Perhaps he fell onto the earth with a silent thud. Or perhaps he can still see an opening in front of him. He rises and falls, falls and rises.

# 6

## Hopes and Departures

Elizabeth, the photographer we encountered in the last chapter, obtained permanent residency in 2017, but she found it difficult to find a job and a secure sense of place. When we met in 2018, I asked what she would like to do now that she had legal status. "I don't know," she said. "After so many years without documents, now that I finally got them, it's such a strange feeling that I really don't know what to do." She described her daily life: "Ups and downs." We still keep in touch and exchange regular messages. Sometimes, she writes that she feels sad and let down by some of her friends. She says that she struggles to find a decent accommodation and would like to move to another apartment. Other times, she says how grateful she is to share a delicious dinner with her friends. Or how lovely it is to get a breath of fresh air and see the trees changing color in the fall. Sometimes, we send each other stills from the animated films of the Japanese director Hayao Miyazaki, which we both love.

Elizabeth's passion for Miyazaki's work started in Colombia when, at ten years of age, she watched the movie *Kiki's Delivery Service*. It was a turning point for her. "Kiki was an inspiration to leave home. It gave me the strength and confidence to do it," she told me. The movie recounts the story of Kiki, a thirteen-year-old girl who has to leave home to complete her training as a witch. One night, she says goodbye to her parents and flies into the unknown on a broomstick given to her by her mother. During her flight, Kiki meets another young witch on a similar journey and asks her, "Is it difficult to settle down?" "Oh yes, a lot can go wrong!" the other says. "But I'm a fortune-teller, so I don't have to worry. What's your skill?" "My only skill," Kiki quietly replies, "is flying." Kiki flies through the night, her scruffy hair flowing in the wind, until she reaches the port city of Kerio and decides to settle there.

But settling can be difficult when your only skill is to keep moving. Kiki doesn't have documents, and she is refused accommodation in every hotel. She wanders in the streets, feeling like an outsider. "Who will accept me for who I am?" she sighs. But the following day, luck is on her side: she meets a kind woman who offers her shelter and food in exchange for working for her bakery. Kiki happily accepts her offer and starts to deliver bread on her broomstick.

Kiki becomes friends with Tombo, a young boy who admires her ability to fly. Yet Kiki maintains an ambivalent relationship with him. She is not sure she can trust him. Her life is so different from his as a young boy who carries his teenage years lightly. For Kiki, life rarely feels light. She struggles to adapt to her new responsibilities and work commitments. One day, she loses a delivery when it falls off her broomstick in the middle of the forest, she misses her appointment with Tombo, and she catches a terrible cold. She retreats to her room, slamming the door behind her. The following morning, the baker offers her a bowl of soup, and Kiki recovers. Throughout the movie, we see Kiki slowly gaining confidence. "You need to trust your spirit," an older friend advises her. Her relationship with Tombo also starts to change. Kiki leaves behind her ambivalence and realizes that she needs him as he needs her. Toward the end of the movie, Tombo has an airship accident and is left hanging from one of the vessel's mooring lines. Kiki rescues him with a spectacular twirl, her flying abilities at the service of her friend.

The story of Kiki is one of a young girl who endures misrecognition and loneliness through desire and belonging. She is sustained by her aspiration to find a better future, however uncertain it may be, and by affective relationships, however ambivalent these relationships may be. I started this chapter with Kiki's story because it constitutes a form of knowledge that is part of the cultural production of young people.[1] It inspired Elizabeth to embark on her migration journey, and it also resonates with the capacity of other young people I met to endure hardships through desires and relationships. I would like to reflect on these issues through brief snapshots from the narratives of three young people: Elizabeth, Luis, and Roberto. I argue that for many of the young people I befriended, ways of enduring and disrupting the constraints of migration control were not to be found in the grandeur of resistance or in clamorous public acts.[2] Instead, at the core of their strength lies the possibility of creating revocable affects and moments of respite. In this last chapter, we will examine the shifting hopes and uncertain desires that young people have for their futures despite their undocumented status. While uncertainty related to the precariousness of migratory status, I suggest that uncertainty ultimately allowed young people to endure the limits of their circumstances and the risk of deportation.

## Growing a Community

Remembering her traumatic past experiences, Elizabeth once told me, "You don't forget. But you have to live with it; you have to survive." Despite the trauma she faced, she found ways to survive, endure, and even grow and flourish. The possibility of coping amid loss was facilitated by the crafting of affective communities across national boundaries—her family in Colombia and her friends in Canada:

> What kept me alive was my family—my brothers, my sisters, my
> aunts—but also, I chose life. I saw myself in different people.

When I saw people on the street or people with no rights, people living illegally, I saw myself in those people. So I gained the strength; I gained the inspiration to live—to be a good person but to also find ways to help people like that. I grew a community in so many ways. I built a community by engaging myself in an organization that helps people and cases like mine so that they can have some justice.

*Growing a community* meant seeing herself in other people, helping others, and becoming actively engaged in her surroundings. Through these acts, Elizabeth found the strength to carry on a life with meaning. Growing a community, she said, was "to choose life." This was also an essential way to be socially and politically recognized as a member of the political community. When her refugee claim in Canada was initially refused, her friends organized public demonstrations, asking the government to reconsider her case. After several months, she was finally granted refugee status on humanitarian and compassionate grounds.

During the months Elizabeth was detained and waiting for the court decision, her friends sent her dozens of cards in solidarity. Once, when I visited her in her new apartment, she showed me those colorful cards, which she had suspended from a cord over her bed. "These cards gave me strength when I was detained and everything seemed lost," she said. Every night, before closing her eyes to sleep, she looked up at them as if they were stars. Though it has been many years since she received refugee status, she still has the cards. They are signs of hope and affection from people who recognized her as one of them, as part of their community.

We can think about these cards as the reversal of Ursula Le Guin's story *The Ones Who Walk Away from Omelas*, which we encountered in chapter 5. In the story, a child was imprisoned in a dark cellar and treated with disdain by the citizens of a city. Elizabeth, by contrast, did not receive contemptuous visits but found company in loving cards coming from the outside to tell her, "We recognize who you are; you belong to us." In important ways, these messages antici- pated the successful mobilization that enabled her to stay in Canada. They were good omens, signs of hope and of being part of a shared community—a community she grew. It is that possibility of recogni- tion that Elizabeth held on to while she was in detention and still holds on to now before falling into sleep.

## Moments of Respite

The power of images and affects is also evoked in the narrative of Luis, a boy from Mexico. At seventeen years old, he migrated to the U.S. without his parents, and after one year living there undocu- mented, he moved to Canada. He sustained himself by working in a plastic factory during the day and in a pub during the night. He lived in a basement apartment with three roommates, also without legal status. When I met him, he was twenty years old and had been recently refused asylum in Canada. He had escaped political violence in his home country—but, he said, "the judge couldn't believe this was happening in Mexico." He continued, "But I know the truth. I am so scared. I don't know what kind of visa I am going to get." He applied for humanitarian protection but had little hope for a positive outcome. He started to have frequent panic attacks and said he "did not feel well." Fears and anxieties occupied his mind: "I was feeling crazy. I was crying. I am scared that they are going to send me back. I am just scared."

The only thing that gave him respite—and even joy—was pho- tography. Like Elizabeth, Luis started to take pictures when he came to Montreal. He asked a friend to lend him some money and bought an expensive Reflex camera. His friends started to ask him to take pic- tures at parties or weddings. What he loved most about photography, he said, was the feeling of making others happy: "I take pictures, and when people see them, they get really happy. And then I am happy.

What makes me happy is that they are happy *because* of me. It is a good feeling. If I can help people, I feel good." He then added with pride and excitement, "Everybody is waiting for my pictures when I go to parties! Next day, everybody sends me text messages: *Let's do the photos like that! We're ready for your photo! Where is my photo? I want to see it!*"

In photography, Luis found a way to give meaning to his life through being connected to others, sensing his friends' happiness, and feeling valued and recognized. This new role offered not only a sense of community but also a temporary respite from everyday fear and uncertainty. It allowed Luis to be somewhere else, if only for a moment. He said, "I like to do photography because I want to just break away from all this and because I am so often thinking about this—it is on my mind." He continued, after a pause, "I try, at least, to forget. When I forget for one second, the next second, my thought is back." The respite that photography gave him was instantaneous, temporary—it was here and now. It helped him ignore, for a moment, his suffering.

## Pushing against the Limits

For other young people, moments of respite and recognition were found in subtle acts of resistance. This is, for instance, the case of Roberto, who we met in chapter 4.

Roberto had been a good student—he was quiet enough to stay under his teachers' radars, he was friendly with his classmates, and he played sports. But when his family received a deportation order, he suddenly started to behave disrespectfully in class. His teacher referred him to a psychologist, but he never went to see one. Roberto said, "They [the teachers] think I have some problems. There are people taking medications, and they said that perhaps I need that too. But I told them, 'No, I don't need that.' So they suggested I see a psychologist, and I told them OK. I always tell them OK, but I've

never been to the psychologist." When I asked why he started to mis-
behave at school, he was silent for a while and then said, "I started
to act up because I have to leave. I said to myself, if I am going to
leave . . . well, then I am going to act up!" While Roberto did not
decide to explicitly come out about his legal status, he partially broke
the invisibility he had maintained until then. With his behavior, he
created a space of relief—an impossible desire for recognition. Misbehaving was a way to oppose both the government's order to deport
his family and his parents' decision to leave Canada. It was an act
attesting that he was physically there and that he no longer respected
his teachers, who represented the state authorities.

We can understand Roberto's behavior as a subtle act of
resistance—what James Scott calls a "hidden transcript."[3] Roberto
pressed against the limits, conveying his anger and "signaling a public breaking of the ritual of subordination."[4] He chose to make his
presence partially visible and voice his desire to have a normal life—a
life where you don't have to push so hard against the limits. In one
of our conversations, Roberto thought about his imminent return
and future:

ROBERTO The only thing I don't like about here is the government
    (*softly laughing*). I think it's just too much. Sometimes, when Mexi-
    cans come here to have a better life, they ask them to have visas to
    work. And they work really hard to have a future. And though these
    people are the ones working the most, it seems that the government
    wants them to return to their country. I think it's not fair that they
    say to people to leave because the government doesn't want them
    here. It's like . . . I don't know how to say this politely, but I find
    this . . . nasty.

FRANCESCA But you can say that.

ROBERTO It really sucks! (*Laughing*) It's not fair that they send people
    back to their country!

FRANCESCA Yes, it really sucks! Are you angry that you're going back?

ROBERTO But not really . . . at the same time yes, but at the same time
no. Because I will try hard to come back. I will put all my efforts
forth. I am going to come back. I think that I'm going to come back
to Canada.

Immigration policies, Roberto said, are "nasty" and "not fair."
In fact, they "really suck," he added with a laugh that was both sub-
versive and wounded. Policies had destabilized his belonging to the
community he had established in his four years in Montreal—an intimate circle that included his girlfriend, friends, and schoolmates. This
was a major second rupture after his family's migration to Canada
and the difficult process of adapting to life here. Yet Roberto wished
to remain in Canada. He wanted to come back one day. He reiterated this desire strongly, despite the unlikelihood that it would ever
be realized. When I spoke to him a few months before his deportation, Roberto told me again, with an air of stubbornness, "My life is
here now."

## Affective Lives

So persistent and yet so fragile are the forces of affective lives: Elizabeth's hope when she received her friends' cards, Luis's joy when
his pictures make someone happy, Roberto's desire to come back
to Canada. They are affective fragments—temporary, revocable,
shifting. And yet despite their revocability, these affects play a vital
role in enabling young people to endure their circumstances through
moments of respite and recognition where they feel part of the communities they are growing.

In his lectures on Spinoza at Vincennes-Saint-Denis, Gilles Deleuze
defines an *affect* as a feeling, which may be hope, joy, pain, fear.[5]
Affects, Deleuze tells us, are modes of thought that work differently

than ideas. Ideas normally represent realities. But affects don't necessarily correspond to something tangible. They can presuppose realities, but they are not reducible to them. He explains, "A pain, a love,
this is not representation. There is the idea of the loved thing, to
be sure, there is an idea of something hoped for but hope as such or
love as such represents nothing, strictly nothing."[6]

Affects are not something definite or achieved. Instead, they are
based on *desires*, which, however unclear and confused they may
be, we long and exist for: "Desire is man's every essence, insofar as
it is conceived to be determined, from any given affection of it, to do
something." Affects, Deleuze says, determine continuous variations
in our force of existing: "There is a continuous variation—and this
is what it means to exist—of the force of existing or of the power
of acting." Affects, in their shifting nature, then constitute what we
call *living*.

Importantly, affects depend on the impacts that others have on
us. In fact, Deleuze suggests we perceive an affect when our body
is modified by the external action of another body. For instance, we
perceive heat because we feel the warmth of the sun on our bodies,
which makes us happy. Or, as in Elizabeth's case, we can rejoice
when we receive a postcard from a friend. When our body encounters
another body—an object, a person, or an image—we experience joy
or sadness, depending on whether it is a good or bad encounter. The
variation of these feelings determines our living. It constitutes our
intensity: our quantity of power, the strength of our force. Deleuze
suggests, "Our power of acting or force of existing is increased or
diminished in a continuous manner, on a continuous line, and this is
what we call affect, it's what we call existing."[7]

Our existence, then, profoundly relies on the possibilities that
affective encounters can open in our lives. These encounters form
relationships that "compose or don't compose. It is the dimension
of affection: composition or decomposition between things." If we
have a good convergence, Deleuze contends, a relationship of love is

formed—and a third individual emerges, which is more than the sum of the two. We feel happy and our power is enhanced. But if we have a bad encounter, our body is affected with sadness. We form relationships that may destabilize, break, and even destroy us.

Thus, our affects are based on indefinite desire—a not-yet. They hinge on our encounters with others (people, objects, and images), which have instantaneous effects on us: something happening here and now. Affects, most importantly, move our existence in shifting waves of intensity. They determine our force of existing and our power of acting.

## Hopes and Desires

Many of the young people I met found their capacity to endure in affects based on desires: for example, the yearning to be recognized as part of a community and to interrupt their undocumented status, if only for a moment. Though these desires were indefinite and ambivalent, they gave young people hope. For Roberto, his wish to remain in Canada did not prevent his deportation. Yet he still hoped that he would come back to Canada one day, unlikely though it was. He persisted in saying that his life was here now: "I don't really want to leave. I want to stay here. I will try hard to come back. I will put forth all my efforts." In his words is a desire both powerful and fragile. A yearning that, to be sure, emerges from the wound of what may soon vanish, from the knowledge of its impossibility.

These stubborn gestures are not straightforward acts of political resistance. Resistance emerges from collective action, from a political claim for something that is owed to us.[8] Affects and desires work in a different way. They are imbricated in a sense of hope that emerges against the likelihood that our wish will ever materialize. There is some despair folded into becoming hopeful: hope often emerges in relation to diminishments and disillusionments, bad encounters that affect us with sadness. The present is always haunted by the fact that, as Gabriel Marcel put it, "the conditions that make it possible to hope are strictly the same as those that make it possible to despair."[9] Roberto's desire emerged precisely from the impossibility of remaining in Canada legally. When I asked if he was angry, he replied ambivalently: "But not really . . . at the same time yes, but at the same time no. Because I will try hard to come back." His stubborn hope, his repetition that "my life is here now," was a way to cope with his pain and powerlessness when confronted with deportation.

In recent decades, scholars have examined how hope shapes our lives. Ernest Bloch, in his book *The Principle of Hope*, proposed a "philosophy of hope," analyzing the influence that utopian visions and daydreams have on the present.[10] For Bloch, hope is a method of knowledge—a fundamental component that guides our ways of knowing and being. Vincent Crapanzano suggests thinking about our hopes as "imaginative horizons" that influence how we experience our being here and how we act in our lives.[11]

Other scholars have argued that hope does not simply orient our future toward an idea of a "good life."[12] In profound ways, hope also points to the limits of our circumstances.[13] Miyazaki, for instance, argues that hope is a "method" that arises from the constraints of human agency and pushes our knowledge toward a not-yet. Marco Di Nunzio, echoing Miyazaki, describes hope as "an embrace of uncertainty"—as an everyday act of living within limits, of navigating poverty, and of opening for oneself the possibility of a better life.[14]

Drawing on these perspectives, I argue that for many young people I met, hoping was a way to deal with the conditions of illegality and deportability. Their hopes were not liberatory, nor did they resolve the fundamental uncertainty and hardships of their lives. They were momentaneous and fleeting. Yet hope paradoxically enabled young people to endure the risk of loss that constantly folded into their lives and relationships. It provided a means of imagining different ways of being here and with others, of what the future might be.[15] It offered a moment of relief, opening up a possibility of recognition: that

Elizabeth might be released from detention, Luis might be granted status, Roberto might one day come back to Canada.

## Communities of Potentiality

Affects and desires are essential spheres of belonging. Young people's desires and hopes are intertwined with affective relationships, instantiating a yearning for recognition as part of a social and political community. Alphonso Lingis reflects on the ways we enter community not only by affirming ourselves but by *exposing* ourselves to others, by being permeable to the ways others make us feel. He suggests that "there is, in the receptivity of our sensitive surfaces, a feeling of being not only informed by the forms but affected by the forces of our environment; this feeling is the pleasure and the pain with which we perceive them."[16] Young people's lives are exposed to different external forces after migration: their undocumented status, which produces everyday suffering and anxiety, but also affective relationships, which open up a sense of community and potentiality.

Kathleen Stewart suggests that the key question that affects raise is not one of meaning but one of potentiality and resonance. She says, "The question they beg is not what they might mean in an order of representations, or whether they are good or bad in an overarching scheme of things, but where they might go and what potential modes of knowing, relating, and attending to things are already somehow present in them in a state of potentiality and resonance."[17] I find Stewart's insights helpful in understanding young people's affects as emerging from desires and hopes that create a force field of existing: both a space of *potentiality* to imagine life otherwise and a space of *resonance* with others.[18] To be sure, these spaces of potentiality and resonance are extremely precarious for young people living undocumented.

Uncertainty, however, does not simply add a layer of instability to their lives. Scholars have often argued that migrant young people are in a permanent state of existential uncertainty, as they can't have an "ontological security": a clear sense of who they are, where they are from, and where they are going.[19] I argue that it is precisely this uncertainty that allows young people to maintain a sense of possibility amid hardship. The shifting nature of young people's desires constitutes a form of agency, enabling them to endure their circumstances.

It is an agency that, however, has little to do with positive ideas of willpower as a conscious and individual domain of choice toward a good life. Agency, Stewart reminds us, is "lived through a series of dilemmas: that action is always a reaction; that the potential to act always include the potential to be acted on, or to submit; that one choice precludes others; that all agency is frustrated and unstable and attracted to the potential in things."[20] In similar ways, the agency that enables young people to endure is found in fragile spaces that still persist.

In this chapter, I have shown that these hopeful spaces can create moments of disruption and subtle forms of resistance: they dislocate present suffering, even if only temporarily.[21] This disruptive force relies on the capacity to open up representations of the future that, by virtue of their appeal, can come to affect the present.[22] These representations may be a thought, a dream, or a totally imaginary entity; may be revocable or transitory; and do not have to be achieved or even exist. Their being in the future suffices to affect young people's present, to make them feel recognized and alive. It is a living future, a potentiality that shapes their present and ways of being. It is more than simple optimism, more than a clear will, more than a not-yet. It is a yearning rather than a being. Through the illusion and potentiality of desire, young people invest life with projects that could be realized or could perhaps not be realized. Undocumented young people are unsure whether the forms of social life they hope for, however tenuous and indefinite these might be, will ever be realized. Yet stubbornly, they persist in holding on to the possibilities of the lives they wish for.

# Conclusion

In February 2017, Montreal City Council unanimously passed a motion declaring Montreal a sanctuary city and pledging that undocumented families would have access to health care and education without the fear of being deported. "We are sending a message that refugees and those without papers are victims and so we have to help them," said the mayor, Denis Coderre, a former federal immigration minister.[1] Coderre explained that the motion emerged as a result of a surge in asylum seekers crossing into Canada from the United States following Donald Trump's restrictive immigration policies.[2] "There are times when as a city you have to set the tone, assess what happens elsewhere and act accordingly," he declared, pointing to the need for more welcoming policies to contrast with the increasingly securitized environment in the United States.[3] Access to services for undocumented migrants would be available in a matter of months, Coderre promised, and immigrant aid groups would be consulted to create new regulations. Yet the motion remained a symbolic gesture of goodwill, and no legislation resulted. Most importantly, it didn't bring about a "Don't Ask, Don't Tell" policy, where all city services and agencies would have refrained from asking about immigration status.[4]

In March 2018, one year after Coderre's declaration, protesters gathered to demonstrate against the deportation of Lucy Francineth

Granados. Her story was similar to many of the stories recounted in this book. She was a single mother who fled her country, Guatemala, after being threatened by criminal gangs. Her asylum claim was refused. She remained in Canada undocumented and financially supported her three children, who lived in Guatemala with their grandmother and depended on the remittances sent by their mother. In 2017, Lucy filed a humanitarian application for permanent residence to regularize her status. In January 2018, a Canada Border Services Agency officer informed her lawyer that her file would not be studied unless she returned to Guatemala. She was arrested and detained. Community organizations said that during her arrest, officers used excessive force, pushing her to the floor and twisting her arm as she tried to reach for her phone.[5] Despite mobilization by solidarity groups like Solidarity Across Borders and No One Is Illegal, Lucy was deported.

In December 2018, the newly elected Mayor Valerie Plante clarified what Lucy's deportation made evident: the promise of a sanctuary city was smoke in the air. The definition was misleading, Plante said, and could create a false sense of security among undocumented migrants. Instead of a sanctuary, Montreal was only a "responsible and engaged" city that would stand up for the rights of newcomers with precarious status yet could not halt deportation proceedings.[6]

## An Ambivalent Recognition

Since Coderre's declared intention of establishing Montreal as a sanctuary city, many of the young people I met during fieldwork have been deported along with their families. Some have obtained permanent residency, while the rest are still struggling with the threat of deportation and are denied access to services. Most are enduring some form of uncertainty. Luis, who we met in chapter 6, tried to return to Canada in 2018, two years after being deported. He was caught at the border and sent back to Mexico. "Maybe I'll try again one day.

Life is difficult here," he told me. He still takes pictures at weddings and parties, and he often posts them on Facebook. Roberto, who we met in chapter 4, sent me a photograph of himself reunited with his grandparents a few months after being deported. In the picture he smiles, despite the challenges that return has certainly entailed.

This book has shown what it means for young people to carry on their lives in uncertainty mode and establish relationships in a city that ambiguously excludes and includes them. The daily uncertainty that young people experience is connected to what Judith Butler defines "state-induced precarity": a condition where specific groups are marginalized and deprived of rights, therefore becoming exposed to vulnerability and violence.[7]

I have shown how this precarity has severe implications not only on individuals' well-being and future prospects. Importantly, it has also repercussions for wider society, including for institutional subjects and community groups who encounter undocumented young people in their daily work. These subjects are confronted with the moral dilemma of recognizing and providing care to individuals who hide their identity for fear of deportation. Drawing on the discordant voices of different subjects (young people, mothers, teachers, school boards, the Ministry of Education), this book has examined how young people often remain bracketed in the ambiguities of the law, which leaves them invisible and not fully recognized. In front of the paradox posed by their double status as children in need of protection *and* undocumented migrants to be rejected, the state leaves young people in a zone of ethical suspension—a zone of waiting as subjects.[8] What are the implications, I ask, of living in a society where young people's suffering continues to remain invisible? Who has the right to be *seen* and to *belong*?

In the story of Omelas, which I recounted in chapter 5, a city is built on systems that necessitate the suffering of a child who is hidden in a basement. It is a story of a child who is held captive, naked in a dark cellar under the buildings of Omelas, a wealthy and seemingly happy city. We don't know the child's name, her story, her identity, or how long she has been imprisoned. The child doesn't speak. Omelas's citizens see her once in their lives—when they reach the age of twelve, and they visit her with disdain. Allen Feldman has argued that in late capitalist societies, we are victims of "cultural anesthesia": a "social capacity to inflict pain upon the Other" and "to render the Other's pain inadmissible to public discourse and culture."[9] Omelas is a culturally anesthetized city: it inflicts pain on a captive child while erasing it from the public gaze. Omelas's citizens face the reality of the child only once in their lives and look at it with contempt. For undocumented young people in Canada, who similarly remain hidden in the margins of society, there aren't public visits of disdain. Instead, young people carry on their lives where they are— at best, ambiguously recognized and, at worst, exposed to injury and deportation.

In this book, I have contended that young people's lived experiences, as well as state attitudes toward them, are shaped by forms of *ambivalence*. This core argument is collapsible into a simple notion: not only the law but the lack of response to the law on undocumented young people create ambivalence in both state agents and young people. To develop this argument, I connect macro and micro dimensions: I show how state actors fail to recognize undocumented young people, and I examine the effects of these institutional failures on young people's lives. Throughout the book, the concepts of ambivalence and structural invisibility connect the macro and micro levels of analysis.

Focusing specifically on the case of access to education, I show how marginality is reproduced not only through explicit policies of exclusion but through what I term *structural invisibility*. I define the latter as norms and practices that are silent and ambiguous, unwritten and discretionary, erasing groups of people at a social, legal, and political level. I have examined how the issue of access to school rests not in explicit policies but in a mosaic of opacity: the silence of families, unwritten school regulations, arbitrary practices, and the apparent ignorance of the Ministry of Education that the problem even exists. Amid this lack of clear policies, young people are excluded altogether from school, or when granted access, they become invisible students—physically present but not officially recognized. Understanding the paradoxes shaping young people's experiences and state attitudes toward them matters deeply, as I will explain in what follows, for both practical and analytical reasons.

## Why Does It Matter?

The narratives in this book serve to counter the cultural anesthesia surrounding undocumented young people by deepening our understanding of the struggles they face and by showing how hostile policies disrupt families, communities, and society. Ethnographic stories focus on the microrealities of individuals, showing the depths and nuances of everyday lives. Policymakers often draw on stories or recount narratives at public events, in town halls, or in interviews with the media to highlight strengths and flaws in governments. When presenting my work at a conference, a policymaker told me, "The stories you presented are both small and big. As policymakers, we need to hear them because people's lived experiences are the center of our work, even if we often forget it." The complexity of each story—so small, so big—can thus be fundamental for policymakers in avoiding reducing people's experiences to simplistic tropes and in understanding them within wider social and political contexts. While the stories recounted in this book are situated and produced in specific contexts and intimate fragments, they are also representative of broader social patterns and narratives.[10] As Susan Bibler Coutin reminds us, ethnographic accounts stand in for a whole: "A particular subset of informants is made to stand in for a society, a particular informant is made to stand for this subset, an interview for this informant is made to stand for the informant, a transcript or notes are made to stand for the interview, and a quote from these notes is made to stand for the entire interview."[11]

The stories presented in this book, then, matter in relation to policy processes and broader sociopolitical contexts. In the late twentieth century, undocumented migration emerged globally because of restrictive policies to control international migration and an increasingly connected market economy.[12] Societies have faced multiple challenges—at the social, economic, and political levels—connected to growing populations living in liminal and precarious statuses.[13] The existing evidence suggests that hostile policies, instead of dissuading people from migrating, have exposed them to vulnerability and injury. Hostile policies made migration routes more deadly and made it extremely difficult for individuals to regularize their status and access social services.[14] Researchers, practitioners, and activists in different countries in the world have expressed concerns about restrictions in access to social services such as health care and education, not only putting forth humanitarian and public health reasons, but also arguing that it is more cost-effective to provide access to services and full citizenship.[15]

The exclusion of young people and children is of particular concern because of the long-lasting negative consequences on children's development and contribution to society and because of the state's duty to protect minors.[16] Young people migrate, alone or with their parents, at early ages and spend their most formative years in the country of arrival, forming complex and contradictory experiences of belonging. They put down roots, forming communities of belonging while also suffering marginalization and being exposed to deportation. These mixed experiences of inclusion and exclusion have detrimental impacts on their lives—increasing feelings of fear, anxiety, and uncertainty and blocking their future prospects and pathways to higher education.[17] The majority of the young people I met in my fieldwork experienced signs of psychological distress, including panic attacks and suicidal thoughts.[18] For them, forced return often means going to an unfamiliar country, enduring the pain of separation from the people they have come to love and care for, and being exposed to high degrees of violence.[19] When deported, young people may also be disenfranchised in their country of origin, becoming de facto stateless.[20]

Ultimately, the policy problem that this book grapples with is not undocumented migration. It is borders—the bordering practices that govern and control diversity through securitization and racialized discourses on belonging.[21] It is borders that deny recognition and rights, make people disappear, and eliminate their suffering from public discourse. It is borders that, Achille Mbembe reminds us, are "dead spaces of non-connection which deny the very idea of a shared humanity, of a planet, the only one we have, that we share together."[22]

## The Gaps in the Law

Understanding how policies ambivalently deny rights and belonging to young people also matters for analytical reasons. The stories recounted in this book critically contribute to theories on illegalization and marginalization. They shed light on the lives of undocumented young people who inhabit a complex position in relation to citizenship. Social dilemmas around exclusion and access to services are particularly acute for undocumented children, stemming from their contradictory status as both vulnerable subjects to protect *and* aliens to reject.[23] As Jacqueline Bhabha reminds us, "Their claim to protection as minors is in tension with their excludability as outsiders. In this sense, their membership in the broader community of citizens, including non-citizen residents and others legally present on the territory, is always marginal and precarious."[24]

Undocumented young people find themselves trapped in two opposing representations—one that looks at them as vulnerable minors deserving protection, another that considers them "illegal." These views, I argue, are anchored in adult-centered perspectives that have historically characterized young people as "semi-citizens," lacking moral agency and thus having fewer political rights.[25] Undocumented young people therefore become removable non-citizens—dependent on their parents' status, subject to deportation, and excluded from social services such as health care and education.

In this book, I have examined the ambiguous exclusion of undocumented young people in the Quebec school system. In this context, illegalization operated in subtle and ambiguous ways: it was situated in the silence of the law, the discretion of schools, and the fear of families.

Many scholars have examined how policies and laws make people "illegal" and "impossible subjects"—aliens whose legal and social existence becomes unattainable.[26] This book complements this literature, which overwhelmingly focuses on the United States, by interrogating the Canadian context, where undocumented migration is less on the public radar and remains an unspoken policy dilemma. I argue that a dominant focus on illegality as a definite sociopolitical construction can obscure how undocumented status can be ambiguously shaped in national contexts other than the U.S. not only through the law but also through its silences and opacities.

To understand these legal opacities, I propose the analytical framework of *structural invisibility*: a social and legal erasure that is instituted by the state through legal gaps, unwritten policies, and unspoken and arbitrary practices that ultimately deny recognition and rights. I argue that structural invisibility constitutes a political strategy in itself—one that ambiguously erases young people from social, political, and legal contexts by avoiding the thorny issue of recognition. This analytical focus means shifting our perspective from the vertical dimension—or how policies make subjects—to a horizontal one to highlight how marginalization works through ambiguous practices and relational modes. Importantly, the concept of structural invisibility can be relevant to understand processes of marginalization not only for undocumented groups but also for other social groups that are cast out of society, in a legal and social void.

## Precarious Belongings

This book asks vital questions about the ambiguous exclusion of undocumented young people. For instance, what are the effects of this invisibility on young people's everyday lives and belonging? How do people cope with the constant act of being misrecognized and the threat of deportation? In addressing these questions, this book showed how contradictory policies—both inclusive and exclusive—produced interstitial spaces of belonging. Young people felt caught in the movements of establishing ties and being misrecognized, of saying and not saying, of being and not being. In chapter 4, Roberto described this tension so: "When I feel sad, I don't speak of this with my friends. I take my time. I don't have to talk of this because I am afraid that they will say that I have to leave and that they will say that it would be good if I left. Things like that. I'm afraid they are going to laugh at me. That they're not going to understand my situation." Migration control shaped, in ambivalent terms, young people's everyday lives and the materiality of their belonging with double binds—resulting from the tension between invisibility (as not being seen by others and not wanting to be seen) and visibility (as a desire for recognition). Scholars often assume a linear trajectory that sees young people's existential insecurity as a condition of being "stuck" in a continuing liminal phase where they fail to be "integrated."[27] My aim here is to provide a more flexible and realistic framework for the complex predicament undocumented young people are caught in. I suggest that contradictory feelings not only place young people in an existential precariousness, but they also enable them to endure the risk of deportation and the pain of separation. Through ambivalence, I argue, young people protect themselves from experiencing the wound of separation and the possibility that being here might suddenly cease.

The stories presented in this book point to psychological dynamics and subtle forms of resistance beyond polarized narratives of victimhood or resistance.[28] Many scholars have emphasized not only how individuals internalize the despair of their status as "illegal" but how they actively resist it. Gonzales and Chavez, for instance, argue that practices of resistance can range "from making small steps to improve their lives through education and training to political activism aimed at immigration reforms to provide a path to citizenship for undocumented immigrants."[29] Sigona also notes that "attentiveness to the role of exogenous factors in shaping the condition of 'illegality' should not construct undocumented migrants as passive and agencyless subjects overdetermined by structural conditions, or undocumentedness as a homogeneous and undifferentiated experience."[30] While young people in Canada have rarely engaged in collective political movements like the DREAMers in the United States, they are still resourceful and resilient. Their acts of resistance are more subtle and silent, found, for instance, in misbehavior in class or in stubbornly carrying on with their desires despite deportation.

Throughout the book, I examined how both agency and structure, resistance and vulnerability, coexist in the same subject, while I have intentionally avoided entering unresolved debates around structure and agency.[31] Such debates often depict these as two opposing forces and portray migrant young people as either vulnerable or agentive subjects. In this book, I adopt a more fruitful approach, thinking of domination as never fully imposed and individual agency as always ill-fitting, particularly in contexts of marginalization. I show the struggles of young people's lives, rendering some of the tensions without entirely resolving them. I argue that at the core of the strength of many of the young people I met lies their capacity to carve out spaces of respite and recognition. Young people temporarily forgot their worries in everyday small acts: taking pictures of natural places, being in the company of a friend or a puppy, looking at a postcard, and simply engaging with the people they loved and the places they were invested in. In these spaces, young people could keep a space of hope for the future. They could still establish a desire for social and political existence: the possibility of something that could be otherwise.

Michael, a fourteen-year-old boy from Jamaica, recounted his greatest dream, drawing a picture of himself as a doctor: "My biggest dream is to become, one day, a doctor and to help people. We left our life in our country because of violence. We had to leave our country because of fear. Now that we live underground without legal status, I am sad to see that same fear in the eyes of my mother. Even if we have to hide, my dream will never change. And it will never change. Even if some people try to stop me from succeeding, I will fight to carry on my dream." It is important to ask ourselves questions about the dreams and possibilities of lives that young people like Michael imagine. How will we listen to them? How will we recognize them? Will they realize or become something? To be sure, these are not only abstract questions. The needs of young people and their families are happening *now*. Their ways of establishing affective relationships and their claims to belong are entangled with their everyday interactions with families, peers, schools, neighborhoods, and cities. Hannah Arendt reminds us that "the primordial and specifically human act must at the same time contain the answer to the question asked of every newcomer: 'Who are you?'"[32] If young people cannot fully disclose who they are, this has inevitable consequences on their lives and consigns them to be invisible subjects. A fundamental dilemma then remains open: How can these young people, and their presence in a city, be recognized as part of a humanity we all share and as social and political subjects of a community of belonging?

# ACKNOWLEDGMENTS

*Ways of Belonging* emerges from my internal voice, which, like all voices, doesn't entirely belong to the speaker. It is a voice that originates from a life entangled with others, from the generosity of people, places, and life itself. This book is mine, as are all its shortcomings, but it also belongs to the people with whom I took this journey.

More than anything, I am deeply grateful to the young people and families who shared their lives and stories. I can't express how thankful I am for your trust. I am aware that in choosing to focus on certain narratives, I neglected others that were equally important. I hope I honored some of your struggles and some of your dreams; I hope they resonate in this book.

I could not have completed this work without the different communities in my life. Many reflections have emerged from ongoing dialogue with mentors, colleagues, and friends. This project was part of a wider study on access to health care for women and children, funded by the Canadian Institutes of Health Research (CIHR) and based at the SHERPA Research Institute, McGill University. This was more than a team; it was an academic home: a space for thinking together and supporting one another, a nurturing office—one that never ran short of chocolate. Many people were important during my time there. My supervisor, Cécile Rousseau, showed me how to do research by creating communities of care. Karine Vanthuyne provided guidance in my ethnographic fieldwork and brought clarity when I felt lost. Lisa Stevenson, with her kind brilliance, opened for me new ways of understanding and writing on uncertainty. I would like to thank other people who offered mentorship during fieldwork: Franco Carnevale, Janet Cleveland, Jill Hanley, Toby Measham, Catherine Montgomery, Mónica Ruiz-Casares. Some colleagues became dear friends and provided much support and laughter: Alexandra Ricard-Guay, Pauline Ngirumpatse, Nicolas Moreau, Annie Jaimes, Liana Chase. *Merci.* Arseli Dokumaci read parts of this book and pushed me to think more than I could alone; your friendship and generosity mean the world to me.

At the University of Turin, where I first studied anthropology, Roberto Beneduce showed me how to occupy both scholarly and advocacy roles. At Columbia University, Elizabeth Povinelli influenced my understanding of the dark sides of recognition. At the University of Oxford and University College London, I would like to thank Elaine Chase and Nando Sigona for their support and critical discussions around migration. Roberto Gonzales has encouraged this book at different stages; his work keeps inspiring me. Other colleagues in the field of migration have accompanied me in different ways: Catherine Allerton, Deborah Boehm, Kathryn Cassidy, Elena Fiddian-Qasmiyeh, Adele Galipo, Annika Lems, Mody Perveez, Yousif Qasmiyeh, Stephen Ruszczyk, Susan Terrio, Francisco Villegas, Sarah Walker, Charles Watters. Thank you to Rachel Humphris, Rebecca Ehata, Semhar Haile, and Francesca Morra for your friendship and sharp minds.

At Northumbria University, Toby Brandon, Sofia Dedotsi, Tom Disney, and Monique Lhussier kept work fun and collaborative. At King's College London, my colleagues have provided a supportive academic home. Thank you to Antonia Dawes, Jenny Driscoll, Sharon Gewirtz, Yasmin Gunaratnam, Aisha Hutchinson, John Owens, and Tania de St Croix. Thank you to Hanna Kienzler for our wild conversations. My friends at *Otherwise Magazine* inspire me to write ethnography in more creative ways: thanks to Orkideh Behrouzan, Letizia

Bonanno, Marco Di Nunzio, Asiya Islam, Emma Lochery, Fatima Raja, and Jose Sherwood Gonzales.

If shared communities have been important to writing this book, so have been resources. The research represented in this book has been possible thanks to different funding from the Canadian Institutes of Health Research, the Migration and Ethnicity in Health Interventions Doctoral Award, and the McGill University Doctoral Award. Excerpts from chapter 2 appeared in *Anthropological Theory* and *Emotion, Space and Society*. Excerpts from chapter 3 appeared in *International Journal of Migration, Health and Social Care*. Excerpts from chapters 4 and 5 appeared in *Anthropological Quarterly*. I wish to thank the editors and anonymous reviewers of these journals for their feedback.

Thank you to Kim Guinta and Carah Naseem at Rutgers University Press for believing in the project and for all the support along the way. Thank you to Fatima Raja for her meticulous copyediting. Thank you to Rabia Farooqui for the beautiful artwork that appears on the book cover.

Thank you to my family, without whom I would be nothing. I am grateful to my sister, my brother, my sister-in-law, my niece, and my nephew. *Grazie*. Thank you to Lusungu for his support, his copyediting skills, and for showing me how to grow love every day. My parents taught me the importance of daring to ask questions and of paying attention to what is not said. In her last years of life, my mother sometimes asked me, "Did you finish writing that book?" but she never saw it completed. This book is dedicated to her.

# NOTES

## INTRODUCTION

1. The demonstration was organized by the Non-Status Women's Collective, a part of the Solidarity Across Borders migrant justice network, on March 8, 2016. The collective sent an open letter to Prime Minister Justin Trudeau to denounce their conditions and ask for their status to be regularized. The letter remained unanswered.

2. I have translated the original speech from French.

3. The word used is *apparaitre*, which means "to appear"—hinting at a ghost that suddenly appears before the eyes of the viewer.

4. Hasselberg 2016, 11.

5. Susan Bibler Coutin also refers to migrants' social non-existence to describe how individuals became "physically present but legally absent, existing in a space outside of society, a space of 'nonexistence,' a space that is not actually 'elsewhere' or beyond borders but that is rather a hidden dimension of social reality" (Coutin 2007, 9). See also Coutin 2005; Galemba 2013; Menjívar 2006.

6. Randall 1987, 471.

7. See Abrego 2014; Dreby 2015; Heidbrink 2014; Boehm 2011; H. Castañeda 2019; Gonzales 2015; Zavella 2011; Allerton 2020; Terrio 2015; Bloch, Sigona, and Zetter 2009; Sigona 2012; Boehm and Terrio 2019; Suárez-Orozco et al. 2011.

8. See J. Bhabha 2011, 2009; Boehm and Terrio 2019.

9. Walker and Leitner 2011; Spencer 2016; Gleeson and Gonzales 2012; Meloni et al. 2014; Ruiz-Casares et al. 2010.

10. Allerton 2018, 1094.

11. Some scholars have referred to "legal invisibility" as the lack of registration of birth certificates, which makes children stateless (Setel et al. 2007; I. Ahmed 2010; Willen 2005). Others have used *invisibility* to describe the condition of exclusion and vulnerability of undocumented young people (Allerton 2020; Wahlström Smith 2018; Kingston 2013; Kronick and Rousseau 2015) and of

individuals in contexts of migration and displacement (Bjarnesen and Turner 2020; Galemba 2013; Carter 2010).

12. J. Bhabha 2011, 19.

13. J. Bhabha 2011, 21.

14. J. Bhabha 2011, 22–23.

15. Lems 2020, 405.

16. In 1982, the U.S. Supreme Court ruling *Plyler v. Doe* established that all children, regardless of immigration status, have a constitutional right to free public K–12 education. For the context and legacy of this landmark case, see Gonzales, Heredia, and Negrón-Gonzales 2015.

17. In many countries, undocumented children remain implicitly excluded from education. In Europe, scholarly and policy research have uncovered a variegated and ambiguous picture (Keith and LeVoy 2015; Lundberg and Strange 2017; de Clerck et al. 2011; Spencer 2016). Only seven European countries make *explicit* reference to allowing undocumented children access to education—Belgium, Bulgaria, Finland, Italy, the Netherlands, Spain, and Sweden. Others, such as the United Kingdom and Poland, refer to the right to education of *all* children. Hungary, Latvia, and Malta require a valid residence permit to access school, thus *implicitly* excluding undocumented children. Research has also highlighted other countries where migration regulations exclude minors without status. For instance, in South Africa, the 2012 Immigration Act prevents undocumented children from accessing school without a valid registration document, in contradiction with state legislation in which education is a right for all children (UNESCO 2018; Opfermann 2020). In Malaysia, the Education Act limits access to free education to Malaysian children, making undocumented children invisible and excluded (Allerton 2018, 2020; Lumayag 2016).

18. An exception is Toronto, which, as a sanctuary city, provides access to social services—including health care and education—to undocumented migrants. However, there are many discrepancies in practice, and many school boards give undocumented children limited access to school (Atak 2019; Hudson, Atak, and Hannan 2017; SPT 2010; F. J. Villegas 2017).

19. F. J. Villegas 2017; de Clerck et al. 2011.

20. See also Heyman 2013; Harrison and Lloyd 2012; Coutin 2003.

21. Mountz 2004, 325.

22. De Genova 2006; Bustamante 1976; Heyman 1999; De Genova 2002; Ngai 2014.

23. Ticktin 2011; Holmes 2013; Galemba 2017.

24. Chavez 2008; Menjívar and Kanstroom 2013.

25. Monforte and Dufour 2011; Goldring, Berinstein, and Bernhard 2009; McDonald 2009; Goldring and Landolt 2013.

26. Media coverage includes different cases of unauthorized entry at the U.S.-Canada border, refugee claimants, human smuggling, or deportation (Bloemraad, de Graauw, and Hamlin 2015; Stack and Wilbur 2021; Gilbert 2013; Mountz 2004). The language of "crisis" has shaped many of these public discourses, showing how undocumented migration is often understood as an exceptional and sporadic phenomenon rather than a structural component of Canadian society.

27. Chavez 2008.

28. See Allerton 2014, 2017; Sigona 2012; Ellis and Stam 2017; Bernhard et al. 2007; Bloch, Sigona, and Zetter 2014; Carbajal and Ljuslin 2010; Opfermann 2020.

29. The theme of the "spectrality" of power has been extensively investigated by Achille Mbembe. He argues that our political present establishes "extreme forms of human life, death, worlds, forms of social existence in which vast populations are subjected to conditions of life that confer upon them the status of living dead (ghosts)" (Mbembe and Mitsch 2003, 1). See also Gordon 2008.

30. Allerton 2018.

31. Blunt 2005, 506. See also Yuval-Davis 2011; Gonzales and Sigona 2017.

32. Van Gennep 1960.

33. This literature has focused particularly on the complex condition of 1.5-generation young people living undocumented—those who were born in one country and grew up as children in another country where they migrated with their families (Portes and Rumbaut 2001; Aleinikoff and Rumbaut 1998; Zavella 2011; Silver 2018). Scholars have particularly focused on the U.S. context, where undocumented status is particularly salient in young people's lives, especially when reaching institutional adulthood (Gonzales 2015, 2011; E. Castañeda 2018; Mallet-García and García-Bedolla 2021). Existing literature has also highlighted how young people's mixed feelings of exclusion and belonging vary depending on national and local contexts, national policies and local regulations, age of arrival, and family ties (Ruszczyk 2021; Silver 2018).

34. Durham 2000; Watters 2008.

35. Menjívar 2006.

36. Gonzales 2015.

37. Abrego 2011; Suárez-Orozco et al. 2011; Chang 2005; Piatt 1988.

38. See, for instance, Gonzales and Chavez 2012; Chavez 1990; Seif 2004; Morrissey 2013.

39. In the United States, the DREAMers movement was started by undocumented young people, most of them Mexican- and U.S.-born youth. The movement is named after the DREAM Act (Development, Relief, and Education for Alien Minors Act) proposals in Congress in 2001, which sought to grant

citizenship to undocumented young people. See Nicholls 2013; Vélez-Vélez and Villarrubia-Mendoza 2019; Nicholls 2021; Gonzales 2008; Negrón-Gonzales 2017. Other scholars have also analyzed experiences of activism and resistance of groups of undocumented individuals, though not specifically focusing on the dimension of age (Kronman and Jönsson 2020; Stierl 2012; McNevin 2006).

40. Foucault 1978, 95–96.

41. Gonzales and Chavez 2012; emphasis mine.

42. Crapanzano 2011; Seymour 2012.

43. For literature on the need to explore migrants' subjectivities and complex psychological dynamics, see Ellis, Gonzales, and Rendón García 2019; Ellis and Stam 2017; Papadopoulos, Stephenson, and Tsianos 2008; Ahmad 2011.

44. Berlant 1991.

45. Anzaldúa 1987; Probyn 1996; Firmat 2012; Ifekwunigwe 1999.

46. Ellis, Gonzales, and Rendón García 2019.

47. "The Migratory Status of the Child and Limited Access to Health Care: Equity and Ethical Challenges," a research study funded by the Canadian Institutes of Health Research (CIHR), research grant number 201355. I was affiliated with this study as a PhD student and project coordinator. The broader aim of this study was to document the health status of this marginalized population and to analyze the ethical, social, and medical dilemmas surrounding their access to health care. This research also had a practical and political goal: it aimed, ultimately, to collaboratively elaborate guidelines for clinicians, institutions, and decision-makers.

48. Düvell, Triandafyllidou, and Vollmer 2010; Suárez-Orozco and Yoshikawa 2013; Markova 2009; Van Liempt and Bilger 2009.

49. Young people were equally split by gender. Interviews were conducted in English and French and were audio-recorded with the participants' verbal consent. Full ethical approval was obtained through the McGill University Health Centre Research Ethics Board and the Health and Social Service Health Centre de la Montagne Research Ethics Board.

50. Experiences of belonging and deportability differed for unaccompanied minors and young people who migrated with parents. While all the young people I met experienced an ambivalent sense of belonging, the presence of parents (in the case of both one- or two-caregiver households) partially buffered the hurdles of illegality and deportability. In the experience of the unaccompanied young people I met in Canada, their increased degree of vulnerability did not yet lead to regularization or recognition on the part of the state. Scholars have further examined the role of family in shaping experiences of undocument-edness and deportability (Dreby 2015; Abrego 2014; Boehm 2012; H. Casta-ñeda 2019) and experiences of belonging for unaccompanied young people

(Heidbrink 2014; Chase and Allsopp 2020; Meloni 2020; Galli 2023; Walker and Gunaratnam 2021).

51. The experiences of the young people and families I worked with resonate with the findings of other research with undocumented groups in Canada (Villegas and Aberman 2019; Aberman, Villegas, and Villegas 2016; Ellis and Stam 2017; Bakan and Stasiulis 2003).

52. McHugh 2000; Foner 2003.

53. Crépeau and Nakache 2006; Ruiz-Casares et al. 2010; Mountz 2010.

## CHAPTER 1    REMOVABLE CHILDREN

1. The expression literally means "being in the loose rope" and can also be roughly translated as "walking on thin ice."

2. I have reviewed fifty court decisions and related legal cases from the Federal Court of Appeal.

3. Pupavac 2001; Aries 1962; Qvortrup 1991.

4. Covell, Howe, and Blokhuis 2018.

5. U.N. General Assembly 1989, art. 3, sec. 1.

6. Menjívar and Perreira 2017; Kronick and Rousseau 2015; Bryan and Denov 2011; J. Bhabha 2014.

7. McDonald 2009; Goldring, Berinstein, and Bernhard 2009; Goldring and Landolt 2013; Crépeau and Nakache 2006.

8. Pashang 2011; P. E. Villegas 2010; Bernhard et al. 2007; Goldring, Berinstein, and Bernhard 2009; Ellis 2015.

9. Goldring, Berinstein, and Bernhard (2009) advocate for the use of "precarious status" to represent multiple and potentially variable forms of non-citizen and non-resident statuses in Canada. Throughout this book, however, I primarily use the term *undocumented* for three reasons. First, the young people I encountered during my fieldwork often define themselves as *undocumented* and don't use the term *precarious*. Second, in most cases, minors having difficulty accessing school or social services are in Canada without legal immigration status for either themselves or their parents or families. The lack of legal documents, rather than their precarious status, is often the main challenge they face in accessing services. Third, I use the term in dialogue with the scholarly literature, which widely adopts it.

10. Khandor et al. 2004; Crépeau and Nakache 2006; Ruiz-Casares et al. 2010; Pratt 2005.

11. Butler 2016, 25.

12. Scholars have examined the racialization of undocumented status, particularly in relation to Latinx groups in the U.S. (Armenta 2017; Menjívar 2021; Rodriguez 2020). Asad L. Asad and Matthew Clair developed the concept

of "racialized legal status" as a "social position based on an ostensibly race-neutral legal classification that disproportionately impacts racial/ethnic minorities" (2018, 19). These perspectives emphasize how specific groups are targets of the social and legal production of illegality. In Canada, the racialization of undocumentedness is less visible in the public discourse because undocumented migration remains at the margins of policy debates and official statistics are not available. However, racialization and racism have historically featured in Canadian migration policies. For instance, there is clear evidence that specific groups, such as Latinx groups, are predominantly targeted by restrictive asylum policies (Gilbert 2013; Young 2018; Villegas and Aberman 2019). Other groups, such as Caribbean migrants, have been racialized and exploited as cheap labor in seasonal agricultural work since the 1950s (Preibisch and Binford 2007; Perry 2012; Smith 2015).

13. Chekaraou Ibrahim and Jian 2019; Young 2018.

14. Bhuyan, Vargas, and Píntín-Perez 2016; Young 2018; García 2006; Amnesty International Canada and Canadian Council for Refugees 2017.

15. Mexican refugee claimants had an 82.9 percent rejection rate overall in 2022 (Immigration and Refugee Board of Canada 2022).

16. Vanthuyne et al. 2013; Ruiz-Casares et al. 2010; Goldring and Landolt 2013.

17. Minister of Justice (Canada) 2001, para 25 (1).

18. CCR, United Church of Canada, and International Bureau for Children's Rights 2008.

19. Affidavit of M. Baker 1997, para. 3.

20. Affidavit of M. Baker 1997, supra note 10, para. 5.

21. Canadian law has long been based on jus soli, under which every child born in Canada is entitled to citizenship. However, a new law amending the Citizenship Act came into effect in 2009, limiting birthright citizenship in two ways. First, Canadian-born children can be entitled to citizenship only if at least one of their parents is a permanent resident or citizen of Canada. Second, Canadian parents cannot transmit their citizenship to generations born overseas after one generation. This means that children born overseas in countries based on jus sanguinis may become stateless. Such restrictions on citizenship have raised many concerns regarding the potential statelessness of children born overseas, the creation of second-class citizens, and the negative impact on individual choices of working or studying outside Canada (Galloway 2009).

22. At the time of *Baker v. Canada*, Canadian law was based on jus soli, according to which every child born in Canada is entitled to citizenship.

23. Cohen 2005; Scheper-Hughes and Sargent 1998; Cohen 2009.

24. Bosniak 2008.

25. J. Bhabha 2014, 2009.

26. Baker v. Canada 1999, 75.

27. Other court decisions have considered, in the case of the deportation of the parent of a Canadian child, that the child's best interest should be only one among many factors immigration officers should acknowledge. See, for instance, *Suresh v. Canada* (Minister of Citizenship and Immigration), 2002 SCC 1, [2002] 1 S.C.R. 3 (CanLII); *Legault v. Canada* (Minister of Citizenship and Immigration), [2002] 4 F.C. 358, [2002] FCA 125 (CanLII). For other court decisions quashing deportation orders involving Canadian children, see also *Onowu v. Canada* (Minister of Citizenship and Immigration), [2015] 473 F.T.R. 288 FC; F. v. N., 2022 SCC 51.

28. Panchoo v. Canada 2000.

29. Rea applied pursuant to subsection 24(1) of the Canadian Charter of Rights and Freedoms, asking to desist from deporting her father until an assessment of her best interests was completed. The case law, however, states that a person seeking a remedy under subsection 24(1) must personally have been a victim of an infringement of their Charter rights, and such a person may not base their application on an infringement of the rights of third parties. The court then ruled that she could not base her application on an infringement of the rights of third parties.

30. Pupavac 2001, 99.

31. Panchoo v. Canada 2000, 11.

32. Panchoo v. Canada 2000, 11.

33. Panchoo v. Canada 2000, 12.

34. Heidbrink 2014; J. Bhabha 2014.

35. Hawthorne v. Canada 2001, 2.

36. Hawthorne v. Canada 2001, 5.

37. Hawthorne v. Canada 2001, 5.

38. Hawthorne v. Canada 2001, 5.

39. The establishment of relational, social, or economic ties does not constitute a sufficient positive ground to waive a removal order. In *Vidal v. Canada*, for instance, Canada's Federal Court pointed out that "economic and establishment situations alone would not normally constitute grounds for a positive humanitarian and compassionate recommendation" (Vidal v. Canada 1991).

40. See Bothe 2013; Schindler 1981.

41. Malkki 1995.

42. Beaney 1997.

43. Beaney 1997, 354.

44. Hawthorne v. Canada 2002, 9.

45. The girl's name has been anonymized here. As the sole applicant and a minor, her identity was also anonymized in the legal case (A.M.R.I. v. K.E.R. 2011).

46. A.M.R.I. v. K.E.R. 2011.

47. A.M.R.I. v. K.E.R. 2011, 90.

48. This is in the case of returns pursuant to the Hague Convention.

49. Other scholars have also shown how humanitarian logics create hierarchies of deservingness and justify politics of exclusion (Fassin 2005; Watters 2007; Holmes and Castañeda 2016; Watson 2009; Kronick and Rousseau 2015).

50. Ticktin 2005.

51. O'Neill 1994, 6.

## CHAPTER 2    HIDDEN TRACES

1. See Düvell, Triandafyllidou, and Vollmer 2010; Fluehr-Lobban 2003; Van Liempt and Bilger 2009.

2. Garber, Hanssen, and Walkowitz 2000; Israel and Hay 2006.

3. Beazley et al. 2009.

4. More militant organizations used a rhetoric of coming out of invisibility and encouraged migrants to publicly speak about their situations. However, many families I met were reluctant to publicly expose themselves and their status, as they were afraid of the repercussions.

5. Rabinow 2007; Borneman and Hammoudi 2009.

6. I carried out in-depth, semi-structured interviews along with a colleague, Alexandra Ricard-Guay, as part of the wider project on access to health care for undocumented women and children. In total, we interviewed eighteen women about their experiences of getting medical care during pregnancy as well as their wider experiences of migration (Rousseau et al. 2014).

7. Militant research has been usually described as activist research committed to social and political change collectively with particular social movements academics are affiliated with (Halvorsen 2015; Choudry 2015). The term is sometimes used more generally to describe research that is politically situated and speaks truth to power, aiming to overcome the distance between researchers and informants (Garelli and Tazzioli 2013; De Genova 2013).

8. There has been a tendency to identify ethical research with advocacy positions that promote social justice and denounce the abuses of power experienced by marginalized populations (Farmer 1999; Choudry 2015; Eikeland 2006). These engaged approaches emerged in the 1980s and 1990s, partially as a response to growing critiques, especially from feminist, postcolonial, and postmodernist movements. These critiques questioned the White male power of knowledge, along with the failure of researchers to accept responsibility for the political implications of their work. However, as important as these perspectives are, they fall short in their simple equation of *good* and *ethical* with *political engagement*. Moreover, the human rights paradigm that frames the advocacy approach remains problematic because it often implies Western

normative moral assumptions and may reinforce imperialistic oppression (Eriksen 2001; Abu Lughod 2002).

9. Willen, Mulligan, and Castañeda 2011; Garelli and Tazzioli 2013; Kronick, Cleveland, and Rousseau 2018; Heyman, Morales, and Núñez 2009.

10. Willen, Mulligan, and Castañeda 2011, 335.

11. McGranahan 2018; Back 2007; Behar 2014.

12. See also Lassiter 2005.

## CHAPTER 3    FAILING TO BE CALLED

1. Like all other names in the book, Rosa and Emiliano are pseudonyms I have given to protect the families' and young people's confidentiality.

2. A few cases of deportations received attention from media and activist groups. In Toronto in 2006, four children were apprehended by immigration officials while attending school and eventually deported (F. J. Villegas 2017). In Montreal in 2014, a teenager was deported when visiting his friends in school. Other families living in Montreal sometimes perceived Toronto as being safer and more welcoming because of its status as a "sanctuary city," and they considered the possibility of moving there.

3. Deportations in schools have happened in different instances in Ontario and Quebec. In Ontario, which is a sanctuary city and has a "Don't Ask, Don't Tell" policy, undocumented children still experience many barriers in accessing education and can be deported in schools (see, for instance, CSP 2008; SPT 2010; F. J. Villegas 2017; P. E. Villegas 2013; F. J. Villegas 2018). It is important to note that in Canada, there isn't a specific data protection regulation related to school similar to the Family Educational Rights and Privacy Act (FERPA) in the U.S., which affords families the right to have some control over the disclosure of personally identifiable information from education records. There are, however, specific health-related and employment regulations that protect individual privacy rights in different provinces such as Ontario, British Columbia, and Quebec.

4. There are no official statistics on undocumented populations in Canada. Estimates range from two hundred thousand to five hundred thousand individuals living in Canada, one-quarter of whom are children, and about a half of the documented population lives in Toronto (Jimenez 2005, 2006; Magalhaes, Carrasco, and Gastaldo 2010; CIMM 2022; Rousseau et al. 2013). It has been estimated that seventy thousand people live undocumented in Montreal (Lemieux 2021). In 2020, the government implemented "The Temporary Public Policy for Out-of-Status Construction Workers" to regularize the status of five hundred long-term construction workers in Toronto (IRCC 2020; on undocumented workers in Toronto, see also Gastaldo, Carrasco, and

Magalhaes 2012). In 2023, a new policy doubled the number of eligible applicants, extending the program to one thousand undocumented workers in the
Toronto area.

5. The issue of deservingness and access to social services for undocumented
migrants has generated considerable scholarship in North America and
Europe in the last few decades (Ruiz-Casares et al. 2013; Magalhaes, Carrasco,
and Gastaldo 2010; Watters 2007). Much of this literature revolves around
questions of deservingness, describing and challenging the ways that policies
and public discourse assess immigrants' entitlement to services (Willen 2011;
Viladrich 2011; Abrego and Gonzales 2010). However, discourses of entitlement are often intertwined with pathways to access in a non-obvious way. For
instance, assessments of deservingness, as stated in policies and laws, may
significantly differ from unwritten practices at local and regional levels (Watters 2011). These practices are often driven by what Lukes (2005a) defines
as "covert preferences": stakes and interests that may not even be voiced,
fully articulated, or written. And yet these concealed stakes may operate, at
a local level, in important ways that are distinct from broader discourses of
illegality at a national level. Moreover, pathways to illegality can be shifting
and fuzzy, bringing into question any clear boundary between legality and
illegality (Bosniak 2008), with some categories of undocumented migrants
being seen as more "deserving" than others (J. Bhabha 2004).

6. Sometimes, schools enrolled children without asking for registration fees,
when young people had their refugee claim refused but were awaiting a decision, on humanitarian and compassionate grounds.

7. Danz 2000, 1006. See also Humphris 2019; Hacker et al. 2015; F. J. Villegas
2017.

8. Danz 2000, 1006.

9. Provincial regulations require only a birth certificate as a proof of identity in
order to access education. This regulation was, however, rarely followed by
most school boards, which also demanded a valid immigration document.

10. Similarly, in the United States, undocumented students are blocked from
accessing higher education. See Abrego and Gonzales 2010.

11. Butler 1997a, 26.

12. Althusser 2014.

13. For Althusser, individuals become subjects under the sovereign call of law by
adopting an automatic behavior. It is the enduring and unquestioned nature
of this behavior, similar to what Bourdieu would call a *habitus*, that makes
the subject occupy a place in society that is assigned to them, preventing the
possibility of deviation or hesitation.

14. Following a Marxist tradition, his critique aimed at debunking how interpellation sustains the reproduction of capitalist relationships. See Lukes 2005b.

15. Butler 1997b, 2.
16. Foucault 2003; Butler 1997b.
17. Du Bois 1989; Butler 1997a.
18. Du Bois 1989, 1.
19. Foucault 2003, 1978; Butler 1997b; Althusser 2014; Butler 1997a; Du Bois 1989.
20. Hacking 1986.
21. De Genova 2006; Bustamante 1976; Heyman 1999; De Genova 2002; Ngai 2014.
22. Ticktin 2011; Holmes 2013; Galemba 2017.
23. Andersson 2014, 12.
24. Andersson 2014, 274.
25. De Genova 2002, 424.
26. De Genova 2002, 424.
27. The critical race scholar Angela Harris suggests that scholars deal with the issue of Black women by placing it in footnotes, as a mere "addition" that doesn't need any further comment and doesn't challenge dominant theories and assumptions (1990).
28. Spivak 1999, 384.
29. One representative of each organization participated in the initial working group, which had a total of nine people involved. Another twelve people involved in community organizations joined the group in the following months over a period of three years. The research team's role, through this entire process, was to organize the meetings, coordinate the working group, and manage communication among members.
30. The working group documented and supported about twenty cases a year. Each time the group was involved, it was successful in getting the child enrolled in school. Here, the research team had a brokering role: we linked clients of community organizations with social workers at community health centers. Our twofold role as researchers affiliated with a community health center or a community organization was essential in this process. The tactics of this horizontal mobilization changed in response to specific cases. In some cases, for instance, when families had the right to access free education but lacked information, we put them in contact with the working group's community legal clinic to reassure them about their rights or support them with their immigration situation. At other times, when a school refused to enroll the child or when the family could not afford to pay the registration fees, we put them in contact with a social worker at a community health center. The social worker met the family and assessed how the denial of education would cause irreparable damage to the child's psychological development and well-being. This professional assessment was used strategically by the family, with the support of the community organization, to advocate

that the Ministry of Education uses its discretionary power to waive registration fees. This process was repeated with a few cases, and though successful
in the cases we followed, it was very onerous for the family and the workers.
Moreover, families often felt exposed by having to present their personal cases
to the Ministry. These actions were based on the individual details of the case,
and while the success rate in having children enrolled was extremely high,
this was by no means guaranteed at the start of any given case.

31. It might be somehow surprising that a Ministry representative joined the
group. When we invited the Ministry, the group was already established and
had mapped practices of access to education in the region. When I invited
Claude to join our meetings, he didn't give a specific rationale for his
participation—he simply said in a brief email that he would attend. At the
first meeting, he said that the Ministry was unaware of the situation and was
interested in knowing more. In addition to the interest in gaining knowledge
about undocumented children, perhaps the Ministry decided to contribute
to the group because it involved other institutional subjects such as school
boards and youth protection agencies.

32. Procedures for access to education were sometimes published on the websites
of school boards, although official institutional policy was not necessarily
communicated to schools.

33. Dubois 2014.

34. Scholarly work on workers' discretion challenges top-down approaches of
the state that view policies as mostly produced by governments and laws and
implemented by state actors.

35. Lipsky 2010, xi.

36. Drawing on Lipsky's reflections on discretion, many scholars have further
examined the role and effects of discretion in street-level bureaucracy (Evans
2016; Kelly 1994; Buffat, Hill, and Hupe 2016). Empirical and ethnographic
work has particularly brought alive the nuances and different meanings of
discretion (e.g., Das and Poole 2004). In her study of Romanian Roma families
in the U.K., Rachel Humphris suggests that welfare policies for marginalized
groups are framed within a "governance through uncertainty," characterized by lack of resources and growing responsibilities for frontline workers
(2019). This produces a critical site of discretion, performed in intimate state
encounters and through workers' moral judgments about who is considered "deserving" (see also Bouagga 2012; Kobelinsky 2015; Makaremi 2009).
Other scholars have highlighted the use of workers' discretion to respond to
the increasing procedural standardization and management culture of welfare
institutions. Karen Broadhurst and her colleagues show how social workers

in child services use discretion not only to create categories of deservingness but also to resist institutional constraints—for instance, to buy time to conduct more thorough assessments of children and families in need (Broadhurst et al. 2010, 317).

37. Sharma and Gupta 2009; Fassin et al. 2015.

38. Mbembe 2019, 102.

39. Mbembe 2019, 102.

40. Ellison 1995, 3.

41. Ellison 1995, 3.

42. Namaste 2000.

43. My argument resonates with those of other scholars who have examined how undocumented migrants, and young people especially, are situated in an impossible space of existence. Susan Bibler Coutin, for instance, analyzes these subtle and ambiguous spaces of exclusion and how they shape the lives of Salvadoran undocumented migrants in the United States (Coutin 2007, 2003). She writes, "Exclusion created territorial gaps—the space occupied by the person deemed to be legally outside of the United States. Thus, for territories to have integrity, territorial disruptions were required" (Coutin 2005, 195). She suggests that processes of illegalization simultaneously produce concealed realities: illegality is a social reality that is hidden and yet known. It creates a space of non-existence where young people are made illegal, and yet they exist in hidden niches of society. As Negrón-Gonzales has observed, there is often a profound disjuncture between youth's "*juridical* identities as undocumented migrants, and their *subjective* identities" as young people growing up in U.S. society (2014, 260). See also F. J. Villegas 2018; Willen 2005; Boehm 2012.

## CHAPTER 4    GETTING USED TO HERE

1. See also De Noronha 2020.

2. Interviews and conversations with young people were conducted in French and English. When interviews were in French, "I am used to here" is my translation for the words "*Je suis habitué ici.*" Other young people, especially from Caribbean countries, used the expression "I am used to here" or "I got used to here" to describe their processes of adaptation and place-making in Quebec. The expression "I got used to here" echoed in the narratives of many young people. They repeated these words during our conversations about their sense of home, their lives in Montreal, and their desire to remain in Canada and resist deportation. Many young people said they had gotten used to here as they reflected on their lives in Canada and on the uncertainty

of their circumstances. Others said these words, with tears in their eyes, when their families received deportation orders. In all cases, they told me they had gotten used to here when they felt that their sense of *here* was on the verge of being shattered.

3. See, for instance, Yarris and Castañeda 2015; Fassin 2001.

4. Other scholars have described how experiences of belonging differ in undocumented and mixed-status families. Joanna Dreby and Heide Castañeda have eloquently shown how illegality enters the intimate lives of families, creating forms of inequality and dependency between parents and children (H. Castañeda 2019; Dreby 2015).

5. The ways in which Roberto remembers his process of adaptation are influenced by retrospective reflection. While some of the young people I met were in the process of falling out of status, others had received their legal status and reflected on their past experiences of illegality. All of them, however, experienced a present of uncertainty even after obtaining legal status.

6. Sayad argues that the spatial contradiction of this double absence is coupled with a temporal contradiction. The latter defines migration as a precarious yet indefinitely prolonged process. Society, in fact, tends to see migrants as temporary "hosts," and on their part, migrants often create myths of return to buffer the hurdles of migration and their debts toward their communities of origin. These contradictions, Sayad argues, help create the very illusions that sustain migration—illusions and myths that are maintained by policies in the countries of origin, host societies, and migrants themselves. Ultimately, these illusions serve the economic interests of both host societies and societies of origin by providing an exploitable labor force.

7. Sayad 2004.

8. De Noronha 2020; Boehm and Terrio 2019.

9. The reflections of the geographer Robert Sack on place are also relevant here. Sack reminds us, "A place requires human agency, is something that may take time to know, and a home especially so" (1997, 16). See also Relph 1976.

10. Basso 1996, 13.

11. Basso 1996, xiv.

12. Annika Lems, in her book *Being-Here: Placemaking in a World of Movement*, also describes the complex and often contradictory everyday lives of her Somali friends in Melbourne as they try to find a sense of place. She writes, "Rather than using displacement as a metaphor for a sense of alienation from society, the stories show the different ways people actively make sense of new, left behind or lost places" (Lems 2018, 20).

13. See Antonsich 2010; Skey and Antonsich 2017; Yuval-Davis 2011.

14. The political theorist Wendy Brown defines as "wounded attachments" the politicized identities that have come to fetishize themselves in their wounded

character and thus lose their emancipatory aim and desire for political action. Her discussion emphasizes the limitations of "identity politics" and the troubling aspects of politicized identities (Brown 1995).

15. Yuval-Davis 2011, 35. While Yuval-Davis analyzes at length the politics of belonging, and she convincingly argues that difficult emotions spring from exclusionary politics, she devotes little attention to defining the complex emotional nature of belonging. She remains primarily interested in the construction and contestation of different politics of belonging. Her central question is how nationalistic, religious, and global discourses shape our collectivities and national projects. She follows a long tradition of sociological theory that makes a distinction between two different kinds of collective projects. There are communities based on personal social interactions and informal values, and there are communities governed by indirect interactions and formal values. For instance, Ferdinand Tonnies distinguishes between *community* and *society*, and Emile Durkheim differentiates *organic* and *mechanical* solidarity. These distinctions are important, but they also reproduce rigid dichotomies—community versus state, affective versus political, informal versus formal, feminine versus masculine.

16. See Antonsich 2010; Skey and Antonsich 2017; Yuval-Davis 2011.

17. Similar discourses on recognition as a process granted by the state, vital to human flourishing, are also developed by Nancy Fraser and Jessica Benjamin, among others (Benjamin 1998; Fraser 2000; Fraser and Honneth 2003). However, recently, a more critical scholarship has explored a darker dimension of recognition: how the politics of recognition often occur on the terms of the most powerful. Scholars have examined how Indigenous groups in Canada and Australia have to conform to standards established by colonial states with which they can never fully identify (Povinelli 2002; Coulthard 2014; Simpson 2014). This is what the anthropologist Elizabeth Povinelli, in her analysis of Australian multiculturalism, terms "the cunning of recognition"—the act of forcing the other into prefabricated molds that impose unattainable views of indigeneity and cultural authenticity. Though in the case of undocumented populations in Canada, there is no attempt at formal political recognition, it is important to keep in mind that recognition carries violent norms about how people are required to belong. The relationship between recognition and belonging is always fraught with tensions and power dynamics.

18. Taylor 1997, 26.

19. An abundant literature has examined how illegality can place and displace individual identity, confining subjects to an endless state of limbo or "liminal legality," a border zone where people live in a permanent state of precarity and are excluded from full citizenship. See, for instance, Chavez 2007; Menjívar and Kanstroom 2013; Mountz et al. 2002; Striffler 2007.

20. Migrant young people occupy a central role in the hybridization and transformation of identities, and they have been often portrayed as torn between multiple cultures and histories, intimately entangled and diametrically opposed. See, for instance, Watters 2008; Nilan and Feixa 2006.

21. Hondagneu-Sotelo and Avila 1997; Suárez-Orozco et al. 2011; Abrego 2014; Boehm 2012.

22. Gonzales 2015.

23. Gonzales, Suárez-Orozco, and Dedios-Sanguineti 2013; E. Castañeda 2018.

24. Young people have been often described as stuck and in a stage of existential insecurity in which they fail to become "incorporated" (see, for instance, Grillo 2007; Sommers 2012).

25. Many scholars have examined the essential role of ambivalence in shaping our relationships and psychic lives (see Levine 1988; Wood 1999; Johnson 1979; Burton 2004; H. Bhabha 2012).

26. Freud was one of the first to use the concept of ambivalence to describe the mixed experiences of unconscious thought. He argues that ambivalence is inherent to any love relationship and stems from the tension between desires and constraints: "It emerges straight out of experiences that imply the threat of the loss of the object" (Freud 2005, 216). In *Totem and Taboo*, Freud further argues that ambivalence is related to the conflicting behavior of an individual toward an object of desire when there is a prohibition or a "taboo." The individual wants to touch the object but may not touch it or may even hate the act of touching it. His theorization is linked with an idea of ambivalence as connected to a process of both *identification* and subconscious *repression* toward the desired object.

27. Bhabha complicates simplistic theorizations on the relationship between the colonizer and the colonized, as described, for instance, by Frantz Fanon in *Black Skin, White Masks* (1986) and by Edward Said in *Orientalism*. For Bhabha, beyond the Black mask projected by the colonizer, there is not an identity but an interpretation that is elusive and ambivalent. The concept of ambivalence, instilled in the process of mimicry, opens new ways of resisting domination and creating solidarity. Bhabha writes, "If the subject of desire is never simply a Myself, then the Other is never simply an It-self, a front of identity truth or misrecognition" (2012, 74).

28. H. Bhabha 1984, 132.

29. Homi Bhabha draws here on the notion of "mimicry" developed by the psychoanalyst Jacques Lacan. Mimicry, Lacan suggests, is like camouflage, where difference is not coherently repressed but deferred. Lacan writes, "Mimicry reveals something in so far as it is distinct from what might be called an itself

that is behind. The effect of mimicry is camouflage. . . . It is not a question of harmonizing with the background, but against a mottled background, of becoming mottled—exactly like the technique of camouflage practiced in human welfare" (1978, 99).

30. On belonging and homemaking, see, for instance, Gibson-Graham 2011; Lobo and Ghosh 2013; Ifekwunigwe 1999; hooks 2009; Ahmed et al. 2003; Rapport and Dawson 1998; Humphris 2019; Lems 2018; Probyn 1996; Firmat 2012; Shams 2020.

31. See, for instance, Coutin 2016; Boehm 2011; Zavella 2011; Allerton 2018; Olwig 2007.

32. Zavella 2011, 8.

33. Zavella 2011, 9.

34. Anzaldúa 1987, 19.

35. The idea of the familiar alien is theorized by Freud in the notion of the "uncanny" (*unheimlich*; literally "un-home-like") as a feeling of something both frightening and familiar, something alien that leads us back to what is known. In German, *heimlich* means both belonging to the house or the family and concealing from others something that is private. The process of *unheimlich* thus unveils something familiar yet hidden. The meanings of *heimlich* and *unheimlich* develop toward an ambivalence. Homi Bhabha mobilizes Freud's concept of the uncanny to describe the state of unhomeliness of (post)colonial subjects. This is not an ontological state of lacking a home but rather a sense of split reality between the home and the world that starts with subjection and displacement. Bhabha writes, "In that displacement the border between home and world becomes confused; and, uncannily, the private and the public become part of each other, forcing upon us a vision that is as divided as it is disorienting" (1997, 450). For Bhabha, as for Freud, the sense of the uncanny is revealed through gaps—what remains hidden, unsaid, unspeakable, unanswered. These gaps, evident in the prefix *un-*, are generated from a repression that is reintegrated in the subject as both terrifying and familiar. Bhabha cites as an example Toni Morrison's novel *Beloved*, where the traumatic memory of the murder of a child by his own mother emerges from the holes of a history of Black infant deaths during slavery, from the holes of things that remain unsaid and unsayable—questions that other slaves and fugitives don't ask.

36. Anzaldúa 1987, 41.

37. Anzaldúa 1987, 20.

## CHAPTER 5    DOUBLE BINDS

1. Willen 2007, 10. Sarah Willen has argued for a critical phenomenological approach to the study of migrant illegality: a three-dimensional perspective on illegality as a form of juridical status, a sociopolitical condition, and a mode of being-in-the-world (2019).

2. The notion of abjectivity has been used to describe the radical exclusion of certain groups of people. Julia Kristeva, in a psychoanalytical register, has referred to the condition of being "abject" as something alien and repulsive, which has been expelled from the body, like corporeal fluids or excrement, and rendered "other." Kristeva describes the abject condition as the experience of exile, the wanderings of "a *stray*" who asks himself, "Where am I?" and finds no place to be. "He is on a journey, during the night, the end of which keeps receding" (Kristeva 1982, 8). Judith Butler further elaborates on the framework of abjection, relating it to the process of making subjects. The abject, what has been expelled as repulsive and rendered other, becomes the object of the subject's repulsion. This process is crucial in "constituting a binary distinction that stabilizes and consolidates the coherent subject" (Butler 1990, 254). These binary oppositions include self and other, us and them, and sustain acts of homophobia, racism, and sexism and radically exclude otherness. Imogen Tyler further calls attention to "abjection as a lived social *process*" to examine forms of violence and social exclusion. She defines abjection as "the action of casting out or down, but [also] the condition of one cast down—that is, the condition of being abject" (Tyler 2013, 4).

   In the field of illegality, scholars have used the concept of abjection to represent the forms of social exclusion and the consequences of being cast off from the nation-state. Willen, for instance, describes illegality as "the catalyst for particular forms of abjectivity" (2007, 11). She suggests that the framework of abjectivity helps us understand "the intimate entanglements of law and state power in the lives of people consigned to abject spaces and sociopolitical conditions" (Willen 2019, 10). Nicholas De Genova terms as "American abjection" a form of racialized transnational identity that conflates the U.S.-Mexican "Chicano" community with the minority status of African American Blackness (2008). The framework of abjectivity has also been employed to describe the experiences of 1.5-generation undocumented Latinx migrants in the United States—that is, young people who arrived here as children. Leo R. Chavez and Roberto Gonzales describe how youth are excluded from the community of citizens and how they "inhabit a liminal space where the boundary between their everyday lives in the nation and their lives as part of the nation is maintained as a way of ensuring their control and social regulation" (2012, 256).

3. In another register, scholars have also described the experience of undocumented status as social and structural suffering. For instance, Seth Holmes examines the consequences of illegality as *sufrimiento* (suffering) on the bodies of Mexican workers in farm labor camps—broken, aching, bent down (2013). This definition of illegality captures the relationships between individual problems and social injustice, focusing on broader social and political determinants of health. See also Quesada, Hart, and Bourgois 2011; Walter, Bourgois, and Loinaz 2004; Willen 2019; Benson 2008; Holmes 2013; Larchanché 2020.

4. This ordinary brutality of death is to be found in different contexts where undocumented migrants are exposed to forms of vulnerability and exploitation. I am thinking here about the deaths of migrants crossing borderlands—deaths that often go unnoticed, have their records go missing, or sometimes become media spectacles (De León 2015; Heller and Pezzani 2014; Vogt 2013). Though smaller in size and scale than the U.S.-Mexico border, the Canada-U.S. border has become increasingly securitized, especially with intensifying cooperation on border security in recent years (see, for instance, Helleiner 2013). Niagara Falls is the major border region where migrants embark on dangerous journeys and have sometimes been found dead. Following the attacks of September 11, 2001, and the bilateral Canada-U.S. 2001 Smart Border Agreement, the Niagara border become more securitized, and specific measures of surveillance, detention, and targeted deportation were implemented (Helleiner 2009; Harvard Law School 2006). Most of the time, however, migrants' deaths take place in hidden niches of institutions and society, where the law is often absent or ambiguous. An example is the death of Francisco Javier Romero, a 39-year-old man from Chile. In 2016, three months after setting off for Canada, he was arrested by the border authorities. He died in detention shortly after his arrest, and the cause of death remained undetermined (Kassam 2016).

5. In migration studies, scholars have often linked migrant deaths to border control and migration governance. See, for instance, McMahon and Sigona 2020; Helleiner 2013; Rygiel 2016; Holmes and Castañeda 2016.

6. Foucault argues that one of the greatest transformations in the nineteenth century is the interest of the state in exercising a new form of power—what he calls "biopolitics" (2003, 1978). While the sovereign power of the king has the right to take life or let live, the biopolitical power of the state instead *makes* people live and *lets* others die. The state *makes* its subjects, aligning them to norms and exercising over them the right to "make" certain people live and "let" others die. At the heart of this new form of politics is the control of the *bios*: the lives and bodies of citizens not merely as individuals but as a population, in a massifying dimension. The body is now considered a social

and political issue and thus must be governed in the processes of birth, death, sexuality, and illness.

7. Foucault 2003, 254. Foucault's analysis is primarily interested in the state control of life rather than of death. He is mostly preoccupied with the crucial question of the control of life and living in its massifying and statistical dimension.

8. See also Bridget Anderson 2013.

9. See Králová 2015; Biehl 2013; Cacho 2012.

10. Mbembe 2003, 57. Achille Mbembe further argues that necropolitics entails different forms of "death-in-life," such as techniques of a "war on life support"—that is, a war against wider social and economic infrastructure. Jasbir Puar analyzes these deadly kinds of biopolitics in Gaza, where injury and what she terms the "right to maim" are deliberate strategies of Israeli warfare and settler colonialism (2017). Recent works by Alexander Weheliye and Mel Chen also complement Foucault's analysis, pointing to the important role of racialization and racism in producing biopolitics of death in colonial regimes (Weheliye 2014; Chen 2012).

11. Agamben 1998.

12. This short story has also been used by Elizabeth Povinelli in her book *Economies of Abandonment* (2011) to explore questions of endurance and social belonging in late liberalism.

13. Le Guin 1973, 5.

14. J. Bhabha 2014.

15. Johnson 1979.

16. Melville was deeply interested in the racial hierarchies and human interactions of maritime encounters—in what he called "the watery part of the world." Interestingly, he was influential among many Black Atlantic intellectuals in the 1950s. Of relevance is the work of the Trinidadian historian and critic C. L. R. James. James was detained on Ellis Island for four months in 1952, and while waiting for deportation and pleading with the U.S. government for citizenship, he wrote an essay on Melville, which was later published as *Mariners, Renegades and Castaways* (2001). In this book, James reads *Moby-Dick* as an anticipation of the brutal and destructive nature that would characterize capitalist societies a century later.

17. Melville 1967, 352.

18. Johnson 1979, 581.

19. Derrida 1992.

20. Melville 1967, 583.

21. Melville 1967, 583.

22. Melville 1967, 587.

23. Johnson 1979, 587–588.

24. Said 1999.
25. Said 1999, xi.
26. Bateson 1972; Bateson et al. 1963.
27. Bateson, speaking in 1969 at the Symposium on the Double Bind at the National Institute of Mental Health, reflected on and expanded his earlier theory, coining the term *transcontextual syndrome* (1972). In his paper, Bateson notes that double-bind theory has helped him most of all with the problem of reification. That is, it has revealed how human behavior, as well as any other animal behavior, is sustained by repeated habits and rules. Such patterns are formed not as conscious thoughts but rather in the form of transformations, images, differences, and ideas. Through the term *transcontextual*, Bateson aims to emphasize the breakages in contextual patterns of communication—that is, in the way we make sense (or fail to) of experience by framing it in the context of internal thoughts or dreams.
28. Bateson further notes, "If this pathology can be warded off or resisted, the total experience may promote creativity" (1972, 282).
29. Binswanger 1993, 85.
30. Binswanger 1993, 102.

## CHAPTER 6   HOPES AND DEPARTURES

1. Rodríguez 2009.
2. In Quebec and Canada, undocumented young people have rarely engaged in large political movements, as the DREAMers have in the United States. In Canada, most of the movements that ask for regularization of undocumented immigrants are organized under the name "No One Is Illegal" and are present in the largest Canadian cities, including Montreal, Toronto, and Vancouver. These movements emerged in Canada as responses to the increased border securitization that followed the attacks of September 11, 2001 (Basok 2009; Nyers and Rygiel 2012). In 2002, for instance, undocumented Algerians organized the Action Committee for non-status Algerians and demonstrated against deportations in their community.
3. J. Scott 1990.
4. J. Scott 1990, 196.
5. See also Ben Anderson 2014; Sianne 2009; S. Ahmed 2004, 2014; Stewart 2007.
6. Deleuze 1978.
7. Deleuze 1978.
8. Nyers and Rygiel 2012; Negrón-Gonzales 2015, 2017; Nicholls 2013.
9. Marcel 1967, 101.
10. Bloch 1986.

11. Crapanzano 2004.
12. Appadurai 2004.
13. Ben Anderson 2014; Marcel 1967.
14. Di Nunzio 2019, 298.
15. Povinelli 2011.
16. Lingis 1994, 18.
17. Stewart 2007, 3.
18. See also Povinelli 2011.
19. Chase 2013; Allsopp, Chase, and Mitchell 2015; Suárez-Orozco et al. 2011.
20. Stewart 2007, 86.
21. Bloch 1986.
22. Aberman, Villegas, and Villegas 2016.

## CONCLUSION

1. Jiwani 2011.
2. Coderre noted that 452 illegal immigrants crossed the border from the United States to Quebec in January—315 more than during the same period last year. During Donald Trump's presidency in the United States, media and policy narratives often attributed the surge in undocumented migration and asylum seekers to the outcome of his administration's restrictive migration policies. However, these simplistic explanations tend to minimize, on the one hand, complex domestic, bilateral, and international factors and, on the other hand, the impact that Canadian restrictive policies have had on the rising number of individuals without legal status. See Leuprecht 2019.
3. Jiwani 2011.
4. The concept of "sanctuary city" refers to a variety of policies and practices in different national contexts (Lippert and Rehaag 2012). While sanctuary cities in Canada and the United States aim to protect undocumented migrants, in the United Kingdom, they involve a more general commitment to welcoming asylum seekers and refugees. Typically, sanctuary cities in North America include "Don't Ask, Don't Tell" policies that prohibit municipal police forces and city service agencies from accessing and disseminating information related to immigration status and deny cooperation with federal immigration authorities unless required by federal or state law. In Canada, Toronto activists launched a similar campaign in 2004 (Moffette and Ridgley 2018; Hudson, Atak, and Hannan 2017; F. J. Villegas 2017). This policy, however, often fails to be implemented, and police services continue to cooperate with federal border enforcement agencies to conduct status checks.
5. Solidarity Across Borders 2018.
6. M. Scott 2018; Chanco 2021.

7. Butler 2016.

8. In this book, one of the core arguments is about the ambiguities of the law in front of undocumented young people. Yet the law can also resolve ambiguity—for instance, by granting immigration status or deporting young people. This happened to many young people and families I met who were either granted permanent residence or ultimately deported. The ambiguity of the law changes and often diminishes as young people become adults and lose their status as minors. While the specific focus of this book is not on the transition into adulthood, other scholars have examined the experiences of undocumented young people becoming adults (Gonzales 2015; Chase and Allsopp 2020; Silver 2018; Cebulko 2014).

9. Feldman 1994, 404. This numbness, Feldman contends, results in "the banishment of disconcerting, discordant, and anarchic sensory presences and agents that undermine the normalizing and often silent premises of everyday life" (404).

10. Strathern 2005; Haraway 1988.

11. Coutin 2005, 203.

12. Mountz 2020; Pratt 2005; Walters et al. 2010; Donato and Massey 2016.

13. Ettinger 2010; Ngai 2014; Goldring, Berinstein, and Bernhard 2009; Gonzales et al. 2019.

14. Harrison and Lloyd 2012; McMahon and Sigona 2020; Atak, Hudson, and Nakache 2018.

15. Academic and advocacy research on hostile policies for undocumented migration have emerged globally—for instance, in China, the United States, Canada, Europe, Malaysia, and South Africa (Ruiz-Casares et al. 2010; Onarheim et al. 2018; Keith and LeVoy 2015; Magalhaes, Carrasco, and Gastaldo 2010; Winters et al. 2018; Mukumbang, Ambe, and Adebiyi 2020; Lumayag 2016; Lin et al. 2015; Hanley and Wen 2017).

16. J. Bhabha 2011.

17. Suárez-Orozco et al. 2011; Gonzales 2015; H. Castañeda 2019; Abrego 2014; Dreby 2015.

18. Stacciarini et al. 2015; Gonzales, Suárez-Orozco, and Dedios-Sanguineti 2013.

19. Boehm and Terrio 2019; De Noronha 2020.

20. J. Bhabha 2011; Bosniak 2008; Prabhat 2019.

21. Yuval-Davis, Wemyss, and Cassidy 2019.

22. Mbembe 2019, 99.

23. Ruiz-Casares et al. 2010; Watters 2008.

24. J. Bhabha 2011, 16.

25. Allerton 2018; J. Bhabha 2014.

26. See, for example, Ngai 2014; De Genova 2002.

27. Alexis Silver, in her research with undocumented youth in North Carolina, has argued that young people are unable to follow a pathway of linear incorporation (2018). She uses the metaphor of "tectonic plates" to highlight how conflicting state, federal, and local policies move young people's experiences in different directions, toward or away from incorporation, creating barriers or alignments. Other scholars have also analyzed how young people develop cultural citizenship and belonging that clash with their lack of status and formal exclusion (Allerton 2020; Muñoz 2018).

28. Sigona 2012; Ellis, Gonzales, and Rendón García 2019; Allerton 2020; Opfermann 2020.

29. Gonzales and Chavez 2012, 259.

30. Sigona 2012, 51.

31. Bakewell 2010; Archer 1995.

32. Arendt 1958, 179.

# REFERENCES

Aberman, Tanya, Francisco Javier Villegas, and Paloma E. Villegas, eds. 2016. *Seeds of Hope: Creating a Future in the Shadows*. Toronto: Life Cycle Books.

Abrego, Leisy J. 2011. "Legal Consciousness of Undocumented Latinos: Fear and Stigma as Barriers to Claims-Making for First and 1.5 Generation Immigrants." *Law & Society Review* 45 (2): 337–370.

———. 2014. *Sacrificing Families: Navigating Laws, Labor, and Love across Borders*. Berkeley, Calif.: Stanford University Press.

Abrego, Leisy J., and R. G. Gonzales. 2010. "Blocked Paths, Uncertain Futures: The Postsecondary Education and Labor Market Prospects of Undocumented Latino Youth." *Journal of Education for Students Placed at Risk* 15 (1–2): 144–157.

Abu Lughod, L. 2002. "Do Muslim Women Really Need Saving? Anthropological Reflections on Cultural Relativism and Its Others." *American Anthropologist* 104 (3): 783–790.

Affidavit of M. Baker. 1997. Baker v. Canada (Minister of Citizenship and Immigration), [1999] 2 S.C.R. 817, Supreme Court of Canada.

Agamben, Giorgio. 1998. *Homo Sacer: Sovereign Power and Bare Life*. Redwood, Calif.: Stanford University Press.

Ahmad, Ali Nobil. 2011. *Masculinity, Sexuality and Illegal Migration: Human Smuggling from Pakistan to Europe*. Burlington, Vt.: Ashgate.

Ahmed, I., ed. 2010. *The Plight of the Stateless Rohingyas: Responses of the State, Society & the International Community*. Dhaka: University Press.

Ahmed, Sara. 2004. "Affective Economies." *Social Text* 22 (2): 117–139.

———. 2014. *Cultural Politics of Emotion*. Edinburgh: Edinburgh University Press.

Ahmed, Sara, Claudia Castañeda, Anne-Marie Fortier, and Mimi Sheller. 2003. *Uprootings/Regroundings: Questions of Home and Migration*. Oxford: Berg.

Aleinikoff, T. A., and R. G. Rumbaut. 1998. "Terms of Belonging: Are Models of Membership Self-Fulfilling Prophecies?" *Georgetown Immigration Law Journal* 13:1–24.

Allerton, Catherine. 2014. "Statelessness and the Lives of the Children of Migrants in Sabah, East Malaysia." *Tilburg Law Review* 19 (1–2): 26–34.

———. 2018. "Impossible Children: Illegality and Excluded Belonging among Children of Migrants in Sabah, East Malaysia." *Journal of Ethnic and Migration Studies* 44 (7): 1081–1097.

———. 2020. "Invisible Children? Non-recognition, Humanitarian Blindness and Other Forms of Ignorance in Sabah, Malaysia." *Critique of Anthropology* 40 (4): 455–470.

Allsopp, Jennifer, Elaine Chase, and Mary Mitchell. 2015. "The Tactics of Time and Status: Young People's Experiences of Building Futures While Subject to Immigration Control in Britain." *Journal of Refugee Studies* 28 (2): 163–182.

Althusser, Louis. 2014. *On the Reproduction of Capitalism: Ideology and Ideological State Apparatuses*. London: Verso Books.

Amnesty International Canada, and Canadian Council for Refugees. 2017. *Contesting the Designation of the US as a Safe Third Country*. Ottawa: Amnesty International Canada.

A.M.R.I. v. K.E.R. 2011. ONCA 417 (CanLII). Court of Appeal for Ontario.

Anderson, Ben. 2014. *Encountering Affect: Capacities, Apparatuses, Conditions*. Farnham, U.K.: Ashgate.

Anderson, Bridget. 2013. *Us and Them? The Dangerous Politics of Immigration Control*. Oxford: Oxford University Press.

Andersson, Ruben. 2014. *Illegality, Inc.: Clandestine Migration and the Business of Bordering Europe*. Berkeley: University of California Press.

Antonsich, Marco. 2010. "Searching for Belonging: An Analytical Framework." *Geography Compass* 4 (6): 644–659.

Anzaldúa, Gloria. 1987. *Borderlands / La Frontera*. San Francisco: Aunt Lute.

Appadurai, Arjun. 2004. "The Capacity to Aspire." In *Culture and Public Action*, edited by R. Vijayendra and M. Walton, 59–84. Stanford, Calif.: Stanford University Press.

Archer, Margaret S. 1995. *Realist Social Theory: The Morphogenetic Approach*. Cambridge: Cambridge University Press.

Arendt, Hannah. 1958. *The Human Condition*. Chicago: University of Chicago Press.

Aries, P. 1962. *Centuries of Childhood: A Social History of Family Life*. New York: Vintage.

Armenta, Amada. 2017. "Racializing Crimmigration: Structural Racism, Colorblindness, and the Institutional Production of Immigrant Criminality." *Sociology of Race and Ethnicity* 3 (1): 82–95.

Asad, Asad L., and Matthew Clair. 2018. "Racialized Legal Status as a Social Determinant of Health." *Social Science & Medicine* 199:19–28.

Atak, Idil. 2019. "Toronto's Sanctuary City Policy: Rationale and Barriers." In *Sanctuary Cities and Urban Struggles*, edited by Jonathan Darling and Harald Bauder, 105–130. Manchester: Manchester University Press.

Atak, Idil, Graham Hudson, and Delphine Nakache. 2018. "The Securitisation of Canada's Refugee System: Reviewing the Unintended Consequences of the 2012 Reform." *Refugee Survey Quarterly* 37 (1): 1–24.

Back, Les. 2007. *The Art of Listening*. Oxford: Berg.

Bakan, Abbie, and Daiva Stasiulis, eds. 2003. *Negotiating Citizenship: Migrant Women in Canada and the Global System*. New York: Palgrave.

Baker v. Canada (Minister of Citizenship and Immigration). 1999. 2 S.C.R. 817. Supreme Court of Canada.

Bakewell, Oliver. 2010. "Some Reflections on Structure and Agency in Migration Theory." *Journal of Ethnic and Migration Studies* 36 (10): 1689–1708.

Basok, Tanya. 2009. "Counter-hegemonic Human Rights Discourses and Migrant Rights Activism in the US and Canada." *International Journal of Comparative Sociology* 50 (2): 183–205.

Basso, Keith H. 1996. *Wisdom Sits in Places: Landscape and Language among the Western Apache*. Albuquerque: University of New Mexico Press.

Bateson, G., D. Jackson, J. Haley, and J. Weakland. 1963. "A Note on the Double Bind." *Family Process* 2 (1): 154–161.

Bateson, Gregory. 1972. "Double Bind, 1969." In *Steps to an Ecology of Mind: Collected Essays in Anthropology, Psychiatry, Evolution and Epistemology*, 276–283. Northvale, N.J.: Jason Aronson.

Beaney, Michael. 1997. *The Frege Reader*. London: Blackwell.

Beazley, Harriot, Sharon Bessell, Judith Ennew, and Roxana Waterson. 2009. "The Right to Be Properly Researched: Research with Children in a Messy, Real World." *Children's Geographies* 7 (4): 365–378.

Behar, Ruth. 2014. *The Vulnerable Observer: Anthropology That Breaks Your Heart*. Boston: Beacon.

Benjamin, Jessica. 1998. *Like Subjects, Love Objects: Essays on Recognition and Sexual Difference*. New Haven, Conn.: Yale University Press.

Benson, Peter. 2008. "El campo: Faciality and Structural Violence in Farm Labor Camps." *Cultural Anthropology* 23 (4): 589–629.

Berlant, L. 1991. *The Anatomy of National Fantasy: Hawthorne, Utopia, and Everyday Life*. Chicago: University of Chicago Press.

Bernhard, Judith K., Luin Goldring, Julie Young, Carolina Berinstein, and Beth Wilson. 2007. "Living with Precarious Legal Status in Canada: Implications for the Well-Being of Children and Families." *Refuge* 24 (2): 101–114.

Bhabha, Homi. 1984. "Of Mimicry and Man: The Ambivalence of Colonial Discourse." *Discipleship: A Special Issue on Psychoanalysis* 28:125–133.

———. 1992. "The World and the Home." *Social Text* 31/32:141–153.

————. 2012. *The Location of Culture*. London: Routledge.

Bhabha, Jacqueline. 2004. "The 'Mere Fortuity' of Birth? Are Children Citizens?" In *Migrations and Mobilities: Citizenship, Border and Gender*, edited by S. Benhabib and J. Resnik, 187–227. New York: New York University Press.

————. 2009. "Arendt's Children: Do Today's Migrant Children Have a Right to Have Rights?" *Human Rights Quarterly* 31 (2): 410–451.

————. 2011. *Children without a State: A Global Human Rights Challenge*. Cambridge, Mass.: MIT Press.

————. 2014. *Child Migration and Human Rights in a Global Age*. Princeton, N.J.: Princeton University Press.

Bhuyan, Rupaleem, Adriana Vargas, and Margarita Píntin-Perez. 2016. "Fleeing Domestic Violence from a 'Safe' Country? Refugee Determination for Mexican Asylum-Seekers in Canada." *Refuge: Canada's Journal on Refugees* 32 (3): 95–107.

Biehl, João. 2013. *Vita: Life in a Zone of Social Abandonment*. Berkeley: University of California Press.

Binswanger, Ludwig. 1993. *Dreams and Existence*. Atlantic Highlands, N.J.: Humanities.

Bjarnesen, Jesper, and Simon Turner, eds. 2020. *Invisibility in African Displacements: From Structural Marginalization to Strategies of Avoidance*. London: Zed Books.

Bloch, A., N. Sigona, and R. Zetter. 2009. *"No Right to Dream": The Social and Economic Lives of Young Undocumented Migrants in Britain*. Paul Hamlyn Foundation, University of Oxford. Refugee Studies Centre, and City University.

————. 2014. *Sans papiers: The Social and Economic Lives of Young Undocumented Migrants*. London: Pluto Press.

Bloch, Ernst. 1986. *The Principle of Hope*. Vol. 3. Cambridge, Mass.: MIT Press.

Bloemraad, Irene, Els de Graauw, and Rebecca Hamlin. 2015. "Immigrants in the Media: Civic Visibility in the USA and Canada." *Journal of Ethnic and Migration Studies* 41 (6): 874–896.

Blunt, Alison. 2005. "Cultural Geography: Cultural Geographies of Home." *Progress in Human Geography* 29 (4): 505–515.

Boehm, Deborah A. 2011. "Here/Not Here: Contingent Citizenship and Transnational Mexican Children." In *Everyday Ruptures: Children, Youth, and Migration in Global Perspective*, edited by C. Coe, D. A. Boehm, R. R. Reynolds, J. M. Hess, and H. Rae-Espinoza, 161–173. Nashville: Vanderbilt University Press.

————. 2012. *Intimate Migrations: Gender, Family, and Illegality among Transnational Mexicans*. New York: New York University Press.

Boehm, Deborah A., and Susan J. Terrio, eds. 2019. *Illegal Encounters: The Effect of Detention and Deportation on Young People*. New York: New York University Press.

Borneman, John, and Abdellah Hammoudi. 2009. *Being There: The Fieldwork Encounter and the Making of Truth*. Berkeley: University of California Press.

Bosniak, Linda. 2008. *The Citizen and the Alien: Dilemmas of Contemporary Membership*. Princeton, N.J.: Princeton University Press.

Bothe, Michael. 2013. *The Handbook of International Humanitarian Law*. Oxford: Oxford University Press.

Bouagga, Yasmine. 2012. "Le métier de conseiller d'insertion et de probation: Dans les coulisses de l'état pénal?" *Sociologie du travail* 54 (3): 317–337.

Broadhurst, Karen, David Wastell, Sue White, Christopher Hall, Sue Peckover, Kellie Thompson, Andrew Pithouse, and Dolores Davey. 2010. "Performing 'Initial Assessment': Identifying the Latent Conditions for Error at the Front-Door of Local Authority Children's Services." *British Journal of Social Work* 40 (2): 352–370.

Brown, Wendy. 1995. *States of Injury: Power and Freedom in Late Modernity*. Princeton, N.J.: Princeton University Press.

Bryan, Catherine, and Myriam Denov. 2011. "Separated Refugee Children in Canada: The Construction of Risk Identity." *Journal of Immigrant & Refugee Studies* 9 (3): 242–266.

Buffat, Aurélien, Michael Hill, and Peter Hupe, eds. 2016. *Understanding Street-Level Bureaucracy*. Bristol: Policy Press.

Burton, Gera C. 2004. *Ambivalence and the Postcolonial Subject: The Strategic Alliance of Juan Francisco Manzano and Richard Robert Madden*. New York: Peter Lang.

Bustamante, J. 1976. "Structural and Ideological Conditions of the Mexican Undocumented Immigration to the United States." *American Behavioral Scientist* 19 (3): 364.

Butler, Judith. 1990. *Gender Trouble and the Subversion of Identity*. New York: Routledge.

———. 1997a. *Excitable Speech: A Politics of the Performative*. New York: Routledge.

———. 1997b. *The Psychic Life of Power: Theories in Subjection*. Stanford, Calif.: Stanford University Press.

———. 2016. *Frames of War: When Is Life Grievable?* New York: Verso Books.

Cacho, Lisa Marie. 2012. *Social Death: Racialized Rightlessness and the Criminalization of the Unprotected*. New York: New York University Press.

Carbajal, Myrian, and Nathalie Ljuslin. 2010. "Jeunes sans-papiers d'Amérique latine en Suisse ou devenir adulte sur fond de recomposition de rôles." *Lien social et politiques*, no. 64, 125–135.

Carter, Donald Martin. 2010. *Navigating the African Diaspora: The Anthropology of Invisibility*. Minneapolis: University of Minnesota Press.

Castañeda, Ernesto. 2018. *A Place to Call Home: Immigrant Exclusion and Urban Belonging in New York, Paris, and Barcelona*. Berkeley: Stanford University Press.

Castañeda, Heide. 2019. *Borders of Belonging: Struggle and Solidarity in Mixed-Status Immigrant Families*. Berkeley: Stanford University Press.

CCR (Canadian Council for Refugees), The United Church of Canada, and International Bureau for Children's Rights. 2008. *The Understanding and Application of "Best Interests of the Child" in H & C Decision-Making by Citizenship and Immigration Canada*. http://ccrweb.ca/files/bicreport.pdf.

Cebulko, Kara. 2014. "Documented, Undocumented, and Liminally Legal: Legal Status during the Transition to Adulthood for 1.5-Generation Brazilian Immigrants." *Sociological Quarterly* 55 (1): 143–167.

Chanco, Cristopher. 2021. "Montréal et les sans-papiers: Les grands oubliés des élections municipales?" *Le Devoir*, November 9, 2021. https://www.ledevoir.com/politique/montreal/646113/montreal-et-les-sans-papiers-les-grands-oublies-des-elections-municipales.

Chang, Cindy. 2005. "Health Care for Undocumented Immigrant Children: Special Members of an Underclass." *Wash. ULQ* 83:1271.

Chase, Elaine. 2013. "Security and Subjective Wellbeing: The Experiences of Unaccompanied Young People Seeking Asylum in the UK." *Sociology of Health & Illness* 35 (6): 858–872.

Chase, Elaine, and Jennifer Allsopp. 2020. *Youth Migration and the Politics of Wellbeing: Stories of Life in Transition*. Bristol: Bristol University Press.

Chavez, Leo R. 1990. "Coresidence and Resistance: Strategies for Survival among Undocumented Mexicans and Central Americans in the United States." *Urban Anthropology and Studies of Cultural Systems and World Economic Development* 19 (1): 31–61.

———. 2007. "The Condition of Illegality." *International Migration* 45 (3): 192–196.

———. 2008. *The Latino Threat: Constructing Immigrants, Citizens, and the Nation*. Stanford, Calif.: Stanford University Press.

Chekaraou Ibrahim, Abdou, and Jisong Jian. 2019. "Understanding the Rise of Mexican Migration to Canada." *Mexican Law Review* 11 (2): 55–90.

Chen, Mel Y. 2012. *Animacies: Biopolitics, Racial Mattering, and Queer Affect*. Durham, N.C.: Duke University Press.

Choudry, Aziz. 2015. *Learning Activism: The Intellectual Life of Contemporary Social Movements*. Toronto: University of Toronto Press.

CIMM (Standing Committee on Citizenship and Immigration). 2022. *Undocumented Populations*. Ottawa: Government of Canada.

Cohen, Elizabeth F. 2005. "Neither Seen nor Heard: Children's Citizenship in Contemporary Democracies." *Citizenship Studies* 9 (2): 221–240.

———. 2009. *Semicitizenship in Democratic Politics*. Cambridge: Cambridge University Press.

Coulthard, Glen Sean. 2014. *Red Skin, White Masks: Rejecting the Colonial Politics of Recognition*. Minneapolis: Minnesota University Press.

Coutin, Susan Bibler. 2003. *Legalizing Moves: Salvadoran Immigrants' Struggle for US Residency*. Ann Arbor: University of Michigan Press.

———. 2005. "Being en route." *American Anthropologist* 107 (2): 195-206.

———. 2007. *Nations of Emigrants: Shifting Boundaries of Citizenship in El Salvador and the United States*. Ithaca, N.Y.: Cornell University Press.

———. 2016. *Exiled Home: Salvadoran Transnational Youth in the Aftermath of Violence*. Durham, N.C.: Duke University Press.

Covell, Katherine, R. Brian Howe, and J. C. Blokhuis. 2018. *The Challenge of Children's Rights for Canada*. Waterloo: Wilfrid Laurier University Press.

Crapanzano, Vincent. 2004. *Imaginative Horizons: An Essay in Literary-Philosophical Anthropology*. Chicago: University of Chicago Press.

———. 2011. *The Harkis: The Wound That Never Heals*. Chicago: University of Chicago Press.

Crépeau, François, and Delphine Nakache. 2006. "Controlling Irregular Immigration in Canada: Reconciling Security Concerns with Human Rights Protection." *IRPP Choices* 12 (1): 1-44.

CSP (Community Social Planning). 2008. *The Right to Learn: Access to Public Education for Non-status Immigrants June*. Toronto: Council of Toronto.

Danz, Sheri. 2000. "A Nonpublic Forum or a Brutal Bureaucracy Advocates' Claims of Access to Welfare Center Waiting Rooms." *New York University Law Review* 75:1004.

Das, Veena, and Deborah Poole, eds. 2004. *Anthropology in the Margins of the State*. Santa Fe: School of American Research Press.

de Clerck, Helene Marie-Lou, Julie Ryngaert, Estelle Carton de Wiart, Marie Verhoeven, Wouter Vandenhole, Paul Mahieu, and Christiane Timmerman. 2011. "Undocumented Children and the Right to Education: Illusory Right or Empowering Lever?" *International Journal of Children's Rights* 19 (4): 613-639.

De Genova, Nicholas. 2002. "Migrant 'Illegality' and Deportability in Everyday Life." *Annual Review of Anthropology* 31 (1): 419-447.

———. 2006. "Working the Boundaries: Race, Space, and 'Illegality' in Mexican Chicago." *Journal of Latin American Anthropology* 11 (1): 192-195.

———. 2008. "'American' Abjection: 'Chicanos,' Gangs, and Mexican/Migrant Transnationality in Chicago." *Aztlán: A Journal of Chicano Studies* 33 (2): 141-174.

———. 2013. "'We Are of the Connections': Migration, Methodological Nationalism, and 'Militant Research.'" *Postcolonial Studies* 16 (3): 250-258.

De León, Jason. 2015. *The Land of Open Graves: Living and Dying on the Migrant Trail*. Berkeley: University of California Press.

Deleuze, Gilles. 1978. *Transcripts on Spinoza's Concept of Affect*. https://www.webdeleuze.com/textes/14.

De Noronha, Luke. 2020. *Deporting "Black Britons": Portraits of Deportation to Jamaica*. Manchester: Manchester University Press.

Derrida, Jacques. 1992. "Force of Law: The Metaphysical Foundation of Authority."
In *Deconstruction and the Possibility of Justice*, edited by Drucilla Cornell,
Michel Rosenfeld, and David Carlson, 91–156. London: Routledge.

Di Nunzio, Marco. 2019. *The Act of Living: Street Life, Marginality, and Development in Urban Ethiopia*. Ithaca, N.Y.: Cornell University Press.

Donato, Katharine M., and Douglas S. Massey. 2016. "Twenty-First-Century Glob-
alization and Illegal Migration." *Annals of the American Academy of Political
and Social Science* 666 (1): 7–26.

Dreby, Joanna. 2015. *Everyday Illegal: When Policies Undermine Immigrant Families*. Berkeley: University of California Press.

Dubois, Vincent. 2014. "The State, Legal Rigor, and the Poor: The Daily Practice of
Welfare Control." *Social Analysis* 58 (3): 38–55.

Du Bois, W. E. B. 1989. *The Souls of Black Folk*. London: Routledge.

Durham, Deborah. 2000. "Youth and the Social Imagination in Africa: Introduction
to Parts 1 and 2." *Anthropological Quarterly* 73 (3): 113–120.

Düvell, Franck, Anna Triandafyllidou, and Bastian Vollmer. 2010. "Ethical Issues
in Irregular Migration Research in Europe." *Population, Space and Place* 16
(3): 227–239.

Eikeland, Olav. 2006. "Condescending Ethics and Action Research: Extended
Review Article." *Action Research* 4 (1): 37–47.

Ellis, Basia D. 2015. "The Production of Irregular Migration in Canada." *Canadian
Ethnic Studies* 47 (2): 93–112.

Ellis, Basia D., Roberto G. Gonzales, and Sarah A. Rendón García. 2019. "The Power
of Inclusion: Theorizing 'Abjectivity' and Agency under DACA." *Cultural
Studies ↔ Critical Methodologies* 19 (3): 161–172.

Ellis, Basia D., and Henderikus J. Stam. 2017. "Cycles of Deportability: Threats,
Fears, and the Agency of 'Irregular' Migrants in Canada." *Migration Studies* 6
(3): 321–344. https://doi.org/10.1093/migration/mnx049.

Ellison, Ralph. 1995. *Invisible Man*. New York: Vintage. 1952.

Eriksen, T. H. 2001. "Between Universalism and Relativism: A Critique of the
UNESCO Concept of Culture." In *Culture and Rights: Anthropological Perspectives*, edited by J. K. Cowan and M. B. Dembour, 127–148. Cambridge: Cambridge University Press.

Ettinger, Patrick. 2010. *Imaginary Lines: Border Enforcement and the Origins of
Undocumented Immigration, 1882–1930*. Austin: University of Texas Press.

Evans, Tony. 2016. *Professional Discretion in Welfare Services: Beyond Street-Level
Bureaucracy*. London: Routledge.

Fanon, Frantz. 1986. *Black Skin, White Masks*. London: Pluto Press.

Farmer, P. 1999. "Pathologies of Power: Rethinking Health and Human Rights."
*American Journal of Public Health* 89 (10): 1486.

Fassin, D. 2001. "The Biopolitics of Otherness: Undocumented Foreigners and Racial Discrimination in French Public Debate." *Anthropology Today* 17 (1): 3–7.

———. 2005. "Compassion and Repression: The Moral Economy of Immigration Policies in France." *Cultural Anthropology* 20 (3): 362–387.

Fassin, Didier, Yasmine Bouagga, Isabelle Coutant, Jean-Sébastien Eideliman, Fabrice Fernandez, Nicolas Fischer, Carolina Kobelinski, Chowra Makaremi, Sarah Mazouz, and Sébastien Roux, eds. 2015. *At the Heart of the State: The Moral World of Institutions*. London: Pluto Press.

Feldman, A. 1994. "On Cultural Anesthesia: From Desert Storm to Rodney King." *American Ethnologist* 21 (2): 404–418.

Firmat, Gustavo Pérez. 2012. *Life on the Hyphen: The Cuban-American Way*. Austin: University of Texas Press.

Fluehr-Lobban, C. 2003. *Ethics and the Profession of Anthropology: Dialogue for Ethically Conscious Practice*. Walnut Creek, Calif.: AltaMira.

Foner, Nancy. 2003. *American Arrivals: Anthropology Engages the New Immigration*. Santa Fe: SAR.

Foucault, M. 1978. *The History of Sexuality: An Introduction*. Vol. 1. New York: Vintage.

———. 2003. *"Society Must Be Defended": Lectures at the Collège de France, 1975–76*. New York: Picador.

Fraser, Nancy. 2000. "Rethinking Recognition." *New Left Review* 3:107.

Fraser, Nancy, and Axel Honneth. 2003. *Redistribution or Recognition? A Political-Philosophical Exchange*. London: Verso.

Freud, S. 2005. *On Murder, Mourning, and Melancholia*. London: Penguin Books.

Galemba, Rebecca. 2013. "Illegality and Invisibility at Margins and Borders." *PoLAR: Political and Legal Anthropology Review* 36 (2): 274–285.

———. 2017. *Contraband Corridor: Making a Living at the Mexico–Guatemala Border*. Stanford, Calif.: Stanford University Press.

Galli, Chiara. 2023. *Precarious Protections: Unaccompanied Minors Seeking Asylum in the US*. Berkeley: University of California Press.

Galloway, Gloria. 2009. "Expats Fear for Children's Fate under New Rules." *Globe and Mail*, February 3, 2009.

Garber, M. B., B. Hanssen, and R. L. Walkowitz. 2000. *The Turn to Ethics*. New York: Brunner-Routledge.

García, María Cristina. 2006. *Seeking Refuge: Central American Migration to Mexico, the United States, and Canada*. Berkeley: University of California Press.

Garelli, Glenda, and Martina Tazzioli. 2013. "Challenging the Discipline of Migration: Militant Research in Migration Studies." *Postcolonial Studies* 16 (3): 245–249.

Gastaldo, Denise, Christine Carrasco, and Lilian Magalhaes. 2012. *Entangled in a Web of Exploitation and Solidarity*. Toronto: University of Toronto Press.

http://www.migrationhealth.ca/sites/default/files/Entangled_in_a_web_of
_exploitation_and_solidarity_LQ.pdf.

Gibson-Graham, J. K. 2011. "A Feminist Project of Belonging for the Anthropocene."
*Gender, Place and Culture* 18 (1): 1–21.

Gilbert, Liette. 2013. "The Discursive Production of a Mexican Refugee Crisis in
Canadian Media and Policy." *Journal of Ethnic and Migration Studies* 39 (5):
827–843.

Gleeson, Shannon, and Roberto G. Gonzales. 2012. "When Do Papers Matter? An
Institutional Analysis of Undocumented Life in the United States." *International
Migration* 50 (4): 1–19. https://doi.org/10.1111/j.1468-2435.2011.00726.x.

Goldring, Luin, Carolina Berinstein, and Judith K. Bernhard. 2009. "Institution-
alizing Precarious Migratory Status in Canada." *Citizenship Studies* 13 (3):
239–265.

Goldring, Luin, and Patricia Landolt. 2013. *Producing and Negotiating Non-citizenship:
Precarious Legal Status in Canada.* Toronto: University of Toronto Press.

Gonzales, Roberto G. 2008. "Left Out but Not Shut down: Political Activism and the
Undocumented Student Movement." *Northwestern Journal of Law & Social
Policy* 3:219.

———. 2011. "Learning to Be Illegal: Undocumented Youth and Shifting Legal Contexts in the Transition to Adulthood." *American Sociological Review* 76 (4):
602–619.

———. 2015. *Lives in Limbo: Undocumented and Coming of Age in America.* Berkeley:
University of California Press.

Gonzales, Roberto G., and Leo Chavez. 2012. "Awakening to a Nightmare: Abjectivity and Illegality in the Lives of Undocumented 1.5-Generation Latino Immigrants in the United States." *Current Anthropology* 53 (3): 255–281.

Gonzales, Roberto G., Luisa L. Heredia, and Genevieve Negrón-Gonzales. 2015.
"Untangling Plyler's Legacy: Undocumented Students, Schools, and Citizenship." *Harvard Educational Review* 85 (3): 318–341.

Gonzales, Roberto G., and Nando Sigona. 2017. *Within and beyond Citizenship:
Borders, Membership and Belonging.* London: Routledge.

Gonzales, Roberto G., Nando Sigona, Martha C. Franco, and Anna Papoutsi,
eds. 2019. *Undocumented Migration.* Cambridge: Polity.

Gonzales, Roberto G., Carola Suárez-Orozco, and Maria Cecilia Dedios-Sanguineti.
2013. "No Place to Belong: Contextualizing Concepts of Mental Health among
Undocumented Immigrant Youth in the United States." *American Behavioral
Scientist* 57 (8): 1174–1199.

Gordon, Avery F. 2008. *Ghostly Matters: Haunting and the Sociological Imagination.*
Minneapolis: University of Minnesota Press.

Grillo, Ralph. 2007. "Betwixt and Between: Trajectories and Projects of Transmigra-
tion." *Journal of Ethnic and Migration Studies* 33 (2): 199–217.

Hacker, Karen, Maria Anies, Barbara L. Folb, and Leah Zallman. 2015. "Barriers to Health Care for Undocumented Immigrants: A Literature Review." *Risk Management Healthcare Policy Review* 8:175–183.

Hacking, Ian. 1986. "Making up People." In *Reconstructing Individualism: Autonomy, Individuality, and the Self in Western Thought*, edited by Thomas C. Heller, Morton Sosna, and David Wellbery, 161–171. Stanford, Calif.: Stanford University Press.

Halvorsen, Sam. 2015. "Militant Research against-and-beyond Itself: Critical Perspectives from the University and Occupy London." *Area* 47 (4): 466–472.

Hanley, Jill, and Ya Wen. 2017. "Social Policy Frameworks of Exclusion: The Challenge of Protecting the Social Rights of 'Undocumented Migrants' in Quebec and Shanghai." *Journal of Asian Public Policy* 10 (3): 249–267.

Haraway, Donna. 1988. "Situated Knowledges: The Science Question in Feminism and the Privilege of Partial Perspective." *Feminist Studies* 14 (3): 575–599.

Harris, Angela. 1990. "Race and Essentialism in Feminist Legal Theory." *Stanford Law Review* 42 (3): 581–616.

Harrison, Jill Lindsey, and Sarah E. Lloyd. 2012. "Illegality at Work: Deportability and the Productive New Era of Immigration Enforcement." *Antipode* 44 (2): 365–385.

Harvard Law School. 2006. "Bordering on Failure: The US Canada Safe Third Country Agreement Fifteen Months after Implementation." http://www.ilw.com/articles/2006,0518-anker.pdf.

Hasselberg, Ines. 2016. *Enduring Uncertainty*. London: Berghahn Books.

Hawthorne v. Canada (Minister of Citizenship and Immigration). 2001. F.C. Federal Court.

Hawthorne v. Canada (Minister of Citizenship and Immigration). 2002. FCA 475. Federal Court of Appeal.

Heidbrink, Lauren. 2014. *Migrant Youth, Transnational Families, and the State: Care and Contested Interests*. Philadelphia: University of Pennsylvania Press.

Helleiner, Jane. 2009. "'As Much American as a Canadian Can Be': Cross-Border Experience and Regional Identity among Young Borderlanders in Canadian Niagara." *Anthropologica* 51 (1): 225–238.

———. 2013. "Unauthorised Crossings, Danger and Death at the Canada–US Border." *Journal of Ethnic and Migration Studies* 39 (9): 1507–1524.

Heller, Charles, and Lorenzo Pezzani. 2014. *Liquid Traces: The Left-to-Die Boat Case*. London: Centre for Research Architecture, Goldsmiths, University of London.

Heyman, Josiah M. C., ed. 1999. *States and Illegal Practices*. London: Berg.

———. 2013. "The Study of Illegality and Legality: Which Way Forward?" *PoLAR: Political and Legal Anthropology Review* 36 (2): 304–307.

Heyman, Josiah McC., Maria Cristina Morales, and Guillermina Gina Núñez. 2009. "Engaging with the Immigrant Human Rights Movement in a Besieged Border

Region: What Do Applied Social Scientists Bring to the Policy Process?" *Napa Bulletin* 31 (1): 13–29.

Holmes, Seth. 2013. *Fresh Fruit, Broken Bodies: Migrant Farmworkers in the United States*. Berkeley: University of California Press.

Holmes, Seth M., and Heide Castañeda. 2016. "Representing the 'European Refugee Crisis' in Germany and Beyond: Deservingness and Difference, Life and Death." *American Ethnologist* 43 (1): 12–24.

Hondagneu-Sotelo, Pierrette, and Ernestine Avila. 1997. "'I'm Here, but I'm There': The Meanings of Latina Transnational Motherhood." *Gender & Society* 11 (5): 548–571.

hooks, bell. 2009. *Belonging: A Culture of Place*. London: Routledge.

Hudson, Graham, Idil Atak, and Charity-Ann Hannan. 2017. "(No) Access TO: A Pilot Study on Sanctuary City Policy in Toronto, Canada." Ryerson Centre for Immigration Settlement Working Paper Series 1, Ryerson University, Toronto.

Humphris, Rachel. 2019. *Home-Land: Romanian Roma, Domestic Spaces and the State*. Bristol: Policy Press.

Ifekwunigwe, Jayne O. 1999. *Scattered Belongings: Cultural Paradoxes of Race, Nation and Gender*. London: Routledge.

Immigration and Refugee Board of Canada. 2022. *Refugee Protection Statistics: Claims by Country of Alleged Persecution*. https://irb.gc.ca/en/statistics/protection/Pages/RPDStat2022.aspx.

IRCC (Immigration, Refugees and Citizenship Canada). 2020. *Temporary Public Policy to Further Facilitate Access to Permanent Resident Status for Out-of-Status Construction Workers in the Greater Toronto Area*. https://www.canada.ca/en/immigration-refugees-citizenship/corporate/mandate/policies-operational-instructions-agreements/further-facilitate-access-permanent-resident-construction-workers-gta.html.

Israel, Mark, and Iain Hay. 2006. *Research Ethics for Social Scientists: Between Ethical Conduct and Regulatory Compliance*. London: Sage.

James, Cyril Lionel Robert. 2001. *Mariners, Renegades and Castaways: The Story of Herman Melville and the World We Live In*. London: University Press of New England.

Jimenez, Marina. 2005. "Broken Gates: Canada's Welcome Mat Frayed and Unravelling." *Globe and Mail*, April 16, 2005. http://migration.ucdavis.edu/rs/more.php?id=158_0_2_0.

———. 2006. "Ottawa Rules Out Amnesty for 200,000 Illegal Workers." *Globe and Mail*, October 27, 2006. https://www.theglobeandmail.com/news/national/ottawa-rules-out-amnesty-for-200000-illegal-workers/article4112345/.

Jiwani, Yasmin. 2011. *Discourses of Denial: Mediations of Race, Gender, and Violence*. Vancouver: University of British Columbia Press.

Johnson, Barbara. 1979. "Melville's Fist: The Execution of 'Billy Budd.'" *Studies in Romanticism* 18 (4): 567–599.

Kassam, Ashifa. 2016. "Immigrant Deaths Expose 'Legal Black Hole' of Canada's Detention System." *Guardian*, May 17, 2016.

Keith, Lilana, and Michele LeVoy. 2015. *Protecting Undocumented Children: Promising Policies and Practices from Governments*. Brussels: PICUM (Platform for International Cooperation on Undocumented Migrants).

Kelly, Marisa. 1994. "Theories of Justice and Street-Level Discretion." *Journal of Public Administration Research and Theory* 4 (2): 119–140.

Khandor, E., J. McDonald, P. Nyers, and C. Wright. 2004. *The Regularization of Non-status Immigrants in Canada, 1960–2004: Past Policies, Current Perspectives, Active Campaigns*. Toronto: Unpublished report prepared for the STATUS Campaign.

Kingston, Lindsey. 2013. "'A Forgotten Human Rights Crisis': Statelessness and Issue (Non)Emergence." *Human Rights Review* 14:73–87.

Kobelinsky, Carolina. 2015. "Judging Intimacies at the French Court of Asylum." *PoLAR: Political and Legal Anthropology Review* 38 (2): 338–355.

Králová, Jana. 2015. "What Is Social Death?" *Contemporary Social Science* 10 (3): 235–248.

Kristeva, Julia. 1982. *Powers of Horror: An Essay on Abjection*. New York: Columbia University Press.

Kronick, Rachel, Janet Cleveland, and Cécile Rousseau. 2018. "'Do You Want to Help or Go to War?': Ethical Challenges of Critical Research in Immigration Detention in Canada." *Journal of Social and Political Psychology* 6 (2): 644–660.

Kronick, Rachel, and Cécile Rousseau. 2015. "Rights, Compassion and Invisible Children: A Critical Discourse Analysis of the Parliamentary Debates on the Mandatory Detention of Migrant Children in Canada." *Journal of Refugee Studies* 28 (4): 544–569.

Kronman, Jenny, and Jessica H. Jönsson. 2020. "We Are Here: Undocumented Migrants and Activism as Resistance." *Critical Radical Social Work* 8 (3): 371-387.

Lacan, Jacques. 1978. *The Line and Light. The Four Fundamental Concepts of Psychoanalysis*. New York: Norton.

Larchanché, Stéphanie. 2020. *Cultural Anxieties: Managing Migrant Suffering in France*. New Brunswick, N.J.: Rutgers University Press.

Lassiter, Luke E. 2005. *The Chicago Guide to Collaborative Ethnography*. Chicago: University of Chicago Press.

Le Guin, Ursula K. 1973. *The Ones Who Walk Away from Omelas*. London: HarperCollins.

Lemieux, François. 2021. "La régularisation du statut des sans papiers résorberait la pénurie de main-d'œuvre." *Metro*, December 4, 2021. https://journalmetro

.com/actualites/montreal/2738806/regulariser-statut-sans-papiers
-permettrait-combler-penurie-main-doeuvre-selon-solidarite-sans-frontieres/.

Lems, Annika. 2018. *Being-Here: Placemaking in a World of Movement*. New York: Berghahn Books.

———. 2020. "Being inside Out: The Slippery Slope between Inclusion and Exclusion in a Swiss Educational Project for Unaccompanied Refugee Youth." *Journal of Ethnic and Migration Studies* 46 (2): 405–422.

Leuprecht, Christian. 2019. *The End of the (Roxham) Road: Seeking Coherence on Canada's Border-Migration Compact*. Ottawa: Macdonald-Laurier Institute.

Levine, Donald N. 1988. *The Flight from Ambiguity: Essays in Social and Cultural Theory*. Chicago: University of Chicago Press.

Lin, Lavinia, Katherine B. Brown, Fan Yu, Jingqi Yang, Jason Wang, Joshua M. Schrock, Adams B. Bodomo, Ligang Yang, Bin Yang, and Eric J. Nehl. 2015. "Health Care Experiences and Perceived Barriers to Health Care Access: A Qualitative Study among African Migrants in Guangzhou, Guangdong Province, China." *Journal of Immigrant and Minority Health* 17 (5): 1509–1517.

Lingis, Alphonso. 1994. *The Community of Those Who Have Nothing in Common*. Bloomington: Indiana University Press.

Lippert, Randy, and Sean Rehaag. 2012. *Sanctuary Practices in International Perspectives: Migration, Citizenship and Social Movements*. London: Routledge.

Lipsky, Michael. 2010. *Street-Level Bureaucracy: Dilemmas of the Individual in Public Services*. New York: Russell Sage Foundation.

Lobo, M., and S. Ghosh. 2013. "Conversations on Belonging: Women of Indian Heritage Speak." *Journal of Intercultural Studies* 34 (4): 410–417.

Lukes, Steven. 2005a. "Power and the Battle for Hearts and Minds." *Millennium: Journal of International Studies* 33 (3): 477–493.

———. (1974) 2005b. *Power: A Radical View*. New York: Palgrave MacMillan.

Lumayag, Linda. 2016. "A Question of Access: Education Needs of Undocumented Children in Malaysia." *Asian Studies Review* 40 (2): 192–210.

Lundberg, Anna, and Michael Strange. 2017. "Struggles over Human Rights in Local Government: The Case of Access to Education for Undocumented Youth in Malmö, Sweden." *Critical Policy Studies* 11 (2): 146–165.

Magalhaes, Lilian, Christine Carrasco, and Denise Gastaldo. 2010. "Undocumented Migrants in Canada: A Scope Literature Review on Health, Access to Services, and Working Conditions." *Journal of Immigrant and Minority Health* 12 (1): 132–151.

Makaremi, Chowra. 2009. "Governing Borders in France: From Extraterritorial to Humanitarian Confinement." *Canadian Journal of Law and Society / La Revue Canadienne Droit et Société* 24 (3): 411–432.

Malkki, Liisa H. 1995. "Refugees and Exile: From 'Refugee Studies' to the National Order of Things." *Annual Review of Anthropology* 24 (1): 495–523.

Mallet-García, Marie L., and Lisa García-Bedolla. 2021. "Immigration Policy and Belonging: Ramifications for DACA Recipients' Sense of Belonging." *American Behavioral Scientist* 65 (9): 1165–1179.

Marcel, G. 1967. "Desire and Hope." In *Readings in Existential Phenomenology*, edited by Daniel O'Connor, 84–112. Englewood Cliffs, N.J.: Prentice-Hall.

Markova, Eugenia. 2009. "The 'Insider' Position: Ethical Dilemmas and Methodological Concerns in Researching Undocumented Migrants with the Same Ethnic Background." In *The Ethics of Migration Research Methodology: Dealing with Vulnerable Immigrants*, edited by Ilse Van Liempt and Veronika Bilger, 141–154. Brighton: Sussex Academic.

Mbembe, Achille. 2003. "Necropolitics." *Public Culture* 15 (1): 11–40.

———. 2019. *Necropolitics*. Durham: Duke University Press.

Mbembe, Achille, and R. H. Mitsch. 2003. "Life, Sovereignty, and Terror in the Fiction of Amos Tutuola." *Research in African Literatures* 34 (4): 1–26.

McDonald, Jean. 2009. "Migrant Illegality, Nation Building, and the Politics of Regularization in Canada." *Refuge: Canada's Journal on Refugees* 26 (2): 65–77.

McGranahan, Carole. 2018. "Ethnography beyond Method: The Importance of an Ethnographic Sensibility." *Sites: A Journal of Social Anthropology* 15 (1). https://doi.org/10.11157/sites-id373.

McHugh, Kevin E. 2000. "Inside, Outside, Upside Down, Backward, Forward, Round and Round: A Case for Ethnographic Studies in Migration." *Progress in Human Geography* 24 (1): 71–89.

McMahon, Simon, and Nando Sigona. 2020. "Death and Migration: Migrant Journeys and the Governance of Migration During Europe's 'Migration Crisis.'" *International Migration Review* 55 (2): 605–628.

McNevin, Anne. 2006. "Political Belonging in a Neoliberal Era: The Struggle of the sans-papiers." *Citizenship Studies* 10 (2): 135–151.

Meloni, Francesca. 2020. "The Limits of Freedom: Migration as a Space of Freedom and Loneliness among Afghan Unaccompanied Migrant Youth." *Journal of Ethnic and Migration Studies* 46 (2): 423–438.

Meloni, Francesca, Cécile Rousseau, Catherine Montgomery, and Toby Measham. 2014. "Children of Exception: Redefining Categories of Illegality and Citizenship in Canada." *Children & Society* 28 (4): 305–315.

Melville, Herman. 1967. *"Billy Budd, Sailor" and Other Stories*. New York: Penguin Books.

Menjívar, Cecilia. 2006. "Liminal Legality: Salvadoran and Guatemalan Immigrants' Lives in the United States." *American Journal of Sociology* 111 (4): 999–1037.

———. 2021. "The Racialization of 'Illegality.'" *Daedalus* 150 (2): 91–105.

Menjívar, Cecilia, and Daniel Kanstroom. 2013. *Constructing Immigrant "Illegality": Critiques, Experiences, and Responses*. Cambridge: Cambridge University Press.

Menjívar, Cecilia, and Krista M. Perreira. 2017. *Undocumented and Unaccompanied: Children of Migration in the European Union and the United States.* London: Routledge.

Minister of Justice (Canada). 2001. Immigration and Refugee Protection Act.

Moffette, David, and Jennifer Ridgley. 2018. "Sanctuary City Organizing in Canada: From Hospitality to Solidarity." *Migration and Society* 1 (1): 147–155.

Monforte, Pierre, and Pascale Dufour. 2011. "Mobilizing in Borderline Citizenship Regimes: A Comparative Analysis of Undocumented Migrants' Collective Actions." *Politics & Society* 39 (2): 203–232.

Morrissey, Megan E. 2013. "A DREAM Disrupted: Undocumented Migrant Youth Disidentifications with US Citizenship." *Journal of International and Intercultural Communication* 6 (2): 145–162.

Mountz, Alison. 2004. "Embodying the Nation-State: Canada's Response to Human Smuggling." *Political Geography* 23 (3): 323–345.

———. 2010. *Seeking Asylum: Human Smuggling and Bureaucracy at the Border.* Minneapolis: University of Minnesota Press.

———. 2020. *The Death of Asylum: Hidden Geographies of the Enforcement Archipelago.* Minneapolis: University of Minnesota Press.

Mountz, Alison, Richard Wright, Ines Miyares, and Adrian J. Bailey. 2002. "Lives in Limbo: Temporary Protected Status and Immigrant Identities." *Global Networks* 2 (4): 335–356.

Mukumbang, Ferdinand C., Anthony N. Ambe, and Babatope O. Adebiyi. 2020. "Unspoken Inequality: How COVID-19 Has Exacerbated Existing Vulnerabilities of Asylum-Seekers, Refugees, and Undocumented Migrants in South Africa." *International Journal for Equity in Health* 19 (1): 1–7.

Muñoz, Susana M. 2018. "Unpacking Legality through La Facultad and Cultural Citizenship: Critical and Legal Consciousness Formation for Politicized Latinx Undocumented Youth Activists." *Equity & Excellence in Education* 51 (1): 78–91.

Namaste, Viviane. 2000. *Invisible Lives: The Erasure of Transsexual and Transgendered People.* Chicago: University of Chicago Press.

Negrón-Gonzales, Genevieve. 2014. "Undocumented, Unafraid and Unapologetic: Re-articulatory Practices and Migrant Youth 'Illegality.'" *Latino Studies* 12 (2): 259–278.

———. 2015. "Undocumented Youth Activism as Counter-spectacle: Civil Disobedience and Testimonio in the Battle around Immigration Reform." *Journal of Chicano Studies* 40 (1): 87–112.

———. 2017. "Political Possibilities: Lessons from the Undocumented Youth Movement for Resistance to the Trump Administration." *Anthropology & Education Quarterly* 48 (4): 420–426.

Ngai, Mae M. 2014. *Impossible Subjects: Illegal Aliens and the Making of Modern America.* Princeton, N.J.: Princeton University Press.

Nicholls, Walter J. 2013. *The DREAMers: How the Undocumented Youth Movement Transformed the Immigrant Rights Debate*. Redwood, Calif.: Stanford University Press.

——. 2021. "The Uneven Geographies of Politicisation: The Case of the Undocumented Immigrant Youth Movement in the United States." *Antipode* 53 (2): 465–485. https://doi.org/10.1111/anti.12663.

Nilan, Pam, and Carles Feixa. 2006. *Global Youth? Hybrid Identities, Plural Worlds*. London: Routledge.

Nyers, Peter, and Kim Rygiel. 2012. *Citizenship, Migrant Activism and the Politics of Movement*. London: Routledge.

Olwig, Karen Fog. 2007. *Caribbean Journeys: An Ethnography of Migration and Home in Three Family Networks*. Durham, N.C.: Duke University Press.

Onarheim, Kristine Husøy, Andrea Melberg, Benjamin Mason Meier, and Ingrid Miljeteig. 2018. "Towards Universal Health Coverage: Including Undocumented Migrants." *BMJ Global Health* 3 (5): 1–6.

O'Neill, J. 1994. *The Missing Child in Liberal Theory: Towards a Covenant Theory of Family, Community, Welfare, and the Civic State*. Toronto: University of Toronto Press; Buffalo: Laidlaw Foundation.

Opfermann, Lena S. 2020. "'If You Can't Beat Them, Be Them!'—Everyday Experiences and 'Performative Agency' among Undocumented Migrant Youth in South Africa." *Children's Geographies* 18 (4): 379–392.

Panchoo v. Canada (Minister of Citizenship and Immigration). 2000. 3-224 Federal Court.

Papadopoulos, Dimitrios, Niamh Stephenson, and Vassilis Tsianos. 2008. *Escape Routes: Control and Subversion in the 21st Century*. London: Pluto Press.

Pashang, S. 2011. "Non-status Women: Invisible Residents and Underground Resilience." PhD diss., Department of Adult Education and Counselling Psychology, University of Toronto.

Perry, J. Adam. 2012. "Barely Legal: Racism and Migrant Farm Labour in the Context of Canadian Multiculturalism." *Citizenship Studies* 16 (2): 189–201.

Piatt, Bill. 1988. "Born as Second Class Citizens in the USA: Children of Undocumented Parents." *Notre Dame L. Rev.* 63:35.

Portes, Alejandro, and Rubén G. Rumbaut. 2001. *Legacies: The Story of the Immigrant Second Generation*. Berkeley: University of California Press.

Povinelli, Elizabeth A. 2002. *The Cunning of Recognition: Indigenous Alterities and the Making of Australian Multiculturalism*. Durham, N.C.: Duke University Press.

——. 2011. *Economies of Abandonment: Social Belonging and Endurance in Late Liberalism*. Durham, N.C.: Duke University Press.

Prabhat, Devyani. 2019. *Citizenship in Times of Turmoil? Theory, Practice and Policy*. London: Edward Elgar.

Pratt, Anna. 2005. *Securing Borders: Detention and Deportation in Canada*. Vancouver: University of British Columbia Press.

Preibisch, Kerry, and Leigh Binford. 2007. "Interrogating Racialized Global Labour Supply: An Exploration of the Racial/National Replacement of Foreign Agricultural Workers in Canada." *Canadian Review of Sociology / Revue Canadienne de Sociologie* 44 (1): 5–36.

Probyn, Elspeth. 1996. *Outside Belongings*. London: Routledge.

Puar, Jasbir K. 2017. *The Right to Maim: Debility, Capacity, Disability*. Durham, N.C.: Duke University Press.

Pupavac, Vanessa. 2001. "Misanthropy without Borders: The International Children's Rights Regime." *Disasters* 25 (2): 95–112.

Quesada, James, Laurie Kain Hart, and Philippe Bourgois. 2011. "Structural Vulnerability and Health: Latino Migrant Laborers in the United States." *Medical Anthropology* 30 (4): 339–362.

Qvortrup, J. 1991. *Childhood as a Social Phenomenon: An Introduction to a Series of National Reports*. Vienna: European Centre.

Rabinow, P. 2007. *Reflections on Fieldwork in Morocco*. Berkeley: University of California Press.

Randall, Margaret. 1987. "Threatened with Deportation." *Latin American Perspectives* 14 (4): 465–479.

Rapport, Nigel, and Andrew Dawson. 1998. *Migrants of Identity: Perceptions of Home in a World of Movement*. Oxford: Berg.

Relph, Edward. 1976. *Place and Placelessness*. London: Pion.

Rodríguez, Ana Patricia. 2009. *Dividing the Isthmus: Central American Transnational Histories, Literatures, and Cultures*. Austin: University of Texas Press.

Rodriguez, Sophia. 2020. "'I Was Born at the Border, like the "Wrong" Side of It': Undocumented Latinx Youth Experiences of Racialization in the US South." *Anthropology & Education Quarterly* 51 (4): 496–526.

Rousseau, Cécile, Audrey Laurin-Lamothe, Joanna Anneke Rummens, Francesca Meloni, Nicolas Steinmetz, and Fernando Alvarez. 2013. "Uninsured Immigrant and Refugee Children Presenting to Canadian Paediatric Emergency Departments: Disparities in Help-Seeking and Service Delivery." *Paediatrics & Child Health* 18 (9): 465–469.

Rousseau, Cécile, Alexandra Ricard-Guay, Audrey Laurin-Lamothe, Anita J. Gagnon, and Hélène Rousseau. 2014. "Perinatal Health Care for Undocumented Women in Montreal: When Sub-standard Care Is Almost the Rule." *Journal of Nursing Education and Practice* 4 (3): 217.

Ruiz-Casares, Mónica, Cécile Rousseau, Ilse Derluyn, Charles Watters, and François Crépeau. 2010. "Right and Access to Healthcare for Undocumented Children: Addressing the Gap between International Conventions and Disparate

Implementations in North America and Europe." *Social Science & Medicine* 70 (2): 329–336.

Ruiz-Casares, Mónica, Cécile Rousseau, Audrey Laurin-Lamothe, Joanna Anneke Rummens, Phyllis Zelkowitz, François Crépeau, and Nicolas Steinmetz. 2013. "Access to Health Care for Undocumented Migrant Children and Pregnant Women: The Paradox between Values and Attitudes of Health Care Professionals." *Maternal and Child Health Journal* 17:292–298.

Ruszczyk, Stephen P. 2021. "Moral Career of Migrant Il/legality: Undocumented Male Youths in New York City and Paris Negotiating Deportability and Regularizability." *Law & Society Review* 55 (3): 496–519.

Rygiel, Kim. 2016. "Dying to Live: Migrant Deaths and Citizenship Politics along European Borders: Transgressions, Disruptions, and Mobilizations." *Citizenship Studies* 20 (5): 545–560.

Sack, Robert David. 1997. *Homo Geographicus: A Framework for Action, Awareness, and Moral Concern*. Baltimore: Johns Hopkins University Press.

Said, Edward W. 1999. *After the Last Sky: Palestinian Lives*. New York: Columbia University Press.

Sayad, A. 2004. *The Suffering of the Immigrant*. Malden, Mass.: Polity.

Scheper-Hughes, N., and C. Sargent. 1998. *Small Wars: The Cultural Politics of Childhood*. Berkeley: University of California Press.

Schindler, Dietrich. 1981. "Human Rights and Humanitarian Law." *Am. UL Rev.* 31:935.

Scott, James C. 1990. *Domination and the Arts of Resistance: Hidden Transcripts*. New Haven, Conn.: Yale University Press.

Scott, Marian. 2018. "Montreal Not a Sanctuary City, but a Responsible One, Plante Says." *Montreal Gazette*, Dec 5, 2018.

Seif, Hinda. 2004. "'Wise Up!' Undocumented Latino Youth, Mexican-American Legislators, and the Struggle for Higher Education Access." *Latino Studies* 2 (2): 210–230.

Setel, Philip W., Sarah B. Macfarlane, Simon Szreter, Lene Mikkelsen, Prabhat Jha, Susan Stout, and Carla AbouZahr. 2007. "A Scandal of Invisibility: Making Everyone Count by Counting Everyone." *Lancet Public Health* 370 (9598): 1569–1577.

Seymour, Claudia. 2012. "Ambiguous Agencies: Coping and Survival in Eastern Democratic Republic of Congo." *Children's Geographies* 10 (4): 373–384.

Shams, Tahseen. 2020. *Here, There, and Elsewhere: The Making of Immigrant Identities in a Globalized World*. Berkeley, Calif.: Stanford University Press.

Sharma, Aradhana, and Akhil Gupta, eds. 2009. *The Anthropology of the State: A Reader*. London: John Wiley & Sons.

Sianne, Ngai. 2009. *Ugly Feelings*. Cambridge, Mass.: Harvard University Press.

Sigona, N. 2012. "'I Have Too Much Baggage': The Impacts of Legal Status on the Social Worlds of Irregular Migrants." *Social Anthropology* 20 (1): 50–65.

Silver, Alexis M. 2018. *Shifting Boundaries: Immigrant Youth Negotiating National, State, and Small-Town Politics.* Berkeley, Calif.: Stanford University Press.

Simpson, Audra. 2014. *Mohawk Interruptus: Political Life across the Borders of Settler States.* Durham, N.C.: Duke University Press.

Skey, Michael, and Marco Antonsich. 2017. *Everyday Nationhood: Theorising Culture, Identity and Belonging after Banal Nationalism.* London: Springer.

Smith, Adrian A. 2015. "Troubling 'Project Canada': The Caribbean and the Making of 'Unfree Migrant Labor.'" *Canadian Journal of Latin American and Caribbean Studies / Revue Canadienne des Études Latino-Américaines et Caraïbes* 40 (2): 274–293.

Solidarity Across Borders. 2018. "Support Rally Thursday for Undocumented Women Violently Arrested, Facing Deportation, in the Sanctuary City of Montreal." March 21. https://www.solidarityacrossborders.org/en/press-releases.

Sommers, Marc. 2012. *Stuck: Rwandan Youth and the Struggle for Adulthood.* Athens: University of Georgia Press.

Spencer, Sarah. 2016. "Postcode Lottery for Europe's Undocumented Children: Unravelling an Uneven Geography of Entitlements in the European Union." *American Behavioral Scientist* 60 (13): 1613–1628.

Spivak, Gayatri Chakravorty. 1999. *A Critique of Postcolonial Reason: Toward a History of the Vanishing Present.* Cambridge, Mass.: Harvard University Press.

SPT (Social Planning Toronto). 2010. *Policy without Practice: Barriers to Enrollment for Non-status Immigrant Students in Toronto's Catholic Schools Produced.* Toronto: Social Planning Toronto.

Stacciarini, Jeanne-Marie R., Rebekah Felicia Smith, Brenda Wiens, Awilda Pérez, Barbara Locke, and Melody LaFlam. 2015. "I Didn't Ask to Come to This Country . . . I Was a Child: The Mental Health Implications of Growing up Undocumented." *Journal of Immigrant and Minority Health* 17 (4): 1225–1230.

Stack, Michelle, and Amea Wilbur. 2021. "Media and Government Framing of Asylum Seekers and Migrant Workers in Canada during the COVID-19 Pandemic." *International Review of Education* 67 (6): 895–914.

Stewart, Kathleen. 2007. *Ordinary Affects.* Durham, N.C.: Duke University Press.

Stierl, Maurice. 2012. "'No One Is Illegal!' Resistance and the Politics of Discomfort." *Globalizations* 9 (3): 425–438.

Strathern, Marilyn. 2005. *Partial Connections.* Walnut Creek, Calif.: AltaMira.

Striffler, Steve. 2007. "Neither Here nor There: Mexican Immigrant Workers and the Search for Home." *American Ethnologist* 34 (4): 674–688.

Suárez-Orozco, C., H. Yoshikawa, R. T. Teranishi, and M. M. Suárez-Orozco. 2011. "Growing up in the Shadows: The Developmental Implications of Unauthorized Status." *Harvard Educational Review* 81 (3): 438–473.

Suárez-Orozco, Carola, and Hirokazu Yoshikawa. 2013. "Undocumented Status: Implications for Child Development, Policy, and Ethical Research." *New Directions for Child and Adolescent Development* 141:61–78.

Taylor, Charles. 1997. "The Politics of Recognition." In *New Contexts of Canadian Criticism*, edited by Ajay Heble, Donna Palmateer Pennee, and J. R. Struthers, 25–73. Peterborough, Ont.: Broadview.

Terrio, Susan J. 2015. *Whose Child Am I?: Unaccompanied, Undocumented Children in US Immigration Custody*. Berkeley: University of California Press.

Ticktin, Miriam. 2005. "Policing and Humanitarianism in France: Immigration and the Turn to Law as State of Exception." *Interventions* 7 (3): 346–368.

———. 2011. *Casualties of Care: Immigration and the Politics of Humanitarianism in France*. Los Angeles: University of California Press.

Tyler, Imogen. 2013. *Revolting Subjects: Social Abjection and Resistance in Neoliberal Britain*. London: Zed Books.

U.N. General Assembly. 1989. Convention on the Rights of the Child.

UNESCO. 2018. *Global Education Monitoring Report Youth Report 2019: Migration, Displacement and Education—Building Bridges, not Walls*. Paris: UNESCO.

van Gennep, Arnold. 1960. *The Rites of Passage*. Chicago: University of Chicago Press.

Van Liempt, Ilse, and Veronika Bilger. 2009. *The Ethics of Migration Research Methodology: Dealing with Vulnerable Immigrants*. Portland, Oreg.: Sussex Academic.

Vanthuyne, Karine, Francesca Meloni, Mónica Ruiz-Casares, Cécile Rousseau, and Alexandra Ricard-Guay. 2013. "Health Workers' Perceptions of Access to Care for Children and Pregnant Women with Precarious Immigration Status: Health as a Right or a Privilege?" *Social Science & Medicine* 93:78–85.

Vélez-Vélez, Roberto, and Jacqueline Villarrubia-Mendoza. 2019. "Interpreting Mobilization Dynamics through Art: A Look at the DREAMers Movement." *Current Sociology* 67 (1): 100–121.

Vidal v. Canada (Minister of Employment and Immigration). 1991. 123, 49 Admin. L.R. 118.

Viladrich, A. 2011. "Beyond Welfare Reform: Reframing Undocumented Immigrants' Entitlement to Health Care in the United States, a Critical Review." *Social Science & Medicine* 74 (6): 822–829.

Villegas, Francisco J. 2017. "'Access without Fear!': Reconceptualizing 'Access' to Schooling for Undocumented Students in Toronto." *Critical Sociology* 43 (7–8): 1179–1195.

———. 2018. "'Don't Ask, Don't Tell': Examining the Illegalization of Undocumented Students in Toronto, Canada." *British Journal of Sociology of Education* 15:1111–1125.

Villegas, Paloma E. 2010. *Mexican Migrants and Immigration Status in Toronto Canada*. Toronto: CERIS.

———. 2013. "Assembling a Visa Requirement against the Mexican 'Wave': Migrant Illegalization, Policy and Affective 'Crises' in Canada." *Ethnic and Racial Studies* 36 (12): 2200–2219.

Villegas, Paloma E., and Tanya Aberman. 2019. "A Double Punishment: The Context of Postsecondary Access for Racialized Precarious Status Migrant Students in Toronto, Canada." *Refuge: Canada's Journal on Refugees / Refuge: Revue Canadienne sur les Réfugiés* 35 (1): 72–82.

Vogt, Wendy A. 2013. "Crossing Mexico: Structural Violence and the Commodification of Undocumented Central American Migrants." *American Ethnologist* 40 (4): 764–780.

Wahlström Smith, Åsa. 2018. "'Hiding in Plain Sight': Daily Strategies and Fear Management among Undocumented Refugee Children in Sweden." *Journal of Refugee Studies* 31 (4): 588–604.

Walker, Kyle E., and Helga Leitner. 2011. "The Variegated Landscape of Local Immigration Policies in the United States." *Urban Geography* 32 (2): 156–178.

Walker, Sarah, and Yasmin Gunaratnam. 2021. "Young, Unauthorised and Black: African Unaccompanied Minors and Becoming an Adult in Italy." *Journal of Sociology* 57 (3): 690–706.

Walter, Nicholas, Philippe Bourgois, and H. Margarita Loinaz. 2004. "Masculinity and Undocumented Labor Migration: Injured Latino Day Laborers in San Francisco." *Social Science & Medicine* 59 (6): 1159–1168.

Walters, William, Galina Cornelisse, Nicholas De Genova, and Nathalie Peutz, eds. 2010. *The Deportation Regime: Sovereignty, Space, and the Freedom of Movement.* Durham, N.C.: Duke University Press.

Watson, Scott D. 2009. *The Securitization of Humanitarian Migration: Digging Moats and Sinking Boats.* London: Routledge.

Watters, C. 2007. "Refugees at Europe's Borders: The Moral Economy of Care." *Transcultural Psychiatry* 44 (3): 394.

———. 2008. *Refugee Children: Towards the Next Horizon.* London: Routledge.

———. 2011. "Towards a New Paradigm in Migrant Health Research: Integrating Entitlement, Access and Appropriateness." *International Journal of Migration, Health and Social Care* 7 (3): 148–159.

Weheliye, Alexander G. 2014. *Habeas Viscus: Racializing Assemblages, Biopolitics, and Black Feminist Theories of the Human.* Durham, N.C.: Duke University Press.

Willen, Sarah. 2005. "Birthing 'Invisible' Children: State Power, NGO Activism, and Reproductive Health among 'Illegal Migrant' Workers in Tel Aviv, Israel." *Journal of Middle East Women's Studies* 1 (2): 55–88.

———. 2007. "Exploring 'Illegal' and 'Irregular' Migrants' Lived Experiences of Law and State Power." *International Migration* 45 (3): 2–27.

———. 2011. "How Is Health-Related 'Deservingness' Reckoned? Perspectives from Unauthorized Im/migrants in Tel Aviv." *Social Science & Medicine* 74 (6): 812–821.

———. 2019. *Fighting for Dignity: Migrant Lives at Israel's Margins*. Philadelphia: University of Pennsylvania Press.

Willen, Sarah S., Jessica Mulligan, and Heide Castañeda. 2011. "Take a Stand Commentary: How Can Medical Anthropologists Contribute to Contemporary Conversations on 'Illegal' Im/migration and Health?" *Medical Anthropology Quarterly* 25 (3): 331–356.

Winters, Marjolein, Bernd Rechel, Lea de Jong, and Milena Pavlova. 2018. "A Systematic Review on the Use of Healthcare Services by Undocumented Migrants in Europe." *BMC Health Services Research* 18 (1): 1–10.

Wood, John Colman. 1999. *When Men Are Women: Manhood among Gabra Nomads of East Africa*. Madison: University of Wisconsin Press.

Yarris, Kristin, and Heide Castañeda. 2015. "Special Issue: Discourses of Displacement and Deservingness: Interrogating Distinctions between 'Economic' and 'Forced' Migration." *International Migration* 53 (3): 64–69.

Young, Julie E. E. 2018. "The Mexico-Canada Border: Extraterritorial Border Control and the Production of 'Economic Refugees.'" *International Journal of Migration and Border Studies* 4 (1–2): 35–50.

Yuval-Davis, Nira. 2011. *The Politics of Belonging: Intersectional Contestations*. London: Sage.

Yuval-Davis, Nira, Georgie Wemyss, and Kathryn Cassidy. 2019. *Bordering*. Cambridge: Polity.

Zavella, Patricia. 2011. *I'm Neither Here nor There: Mexicans' Quotidian Struggles with Migration and Poverty*. Durham, N.C.: Duke University Press.

# INDEX

abjectivity, 10, 82, 142n2
adaptation process (following migration), 65–66, 103, 138n5; "used to here" (expression), 62, 64, 70–72, 75, 78, 137n2
adulthood, 9, 74, 84, 127n33, 147n8
affects, 67, 98, 100, 103–105, 107
agency, 11, 12, 79, 106, 118, 138n9; moral, 26, 33, 116; potentiality, 108; relationship end, 63; and resistance, 9, 10, 11; unaccompanied minors, 85–86; and vulnerability, 86, 87–88, 118
alien (term), 5, 45, 77, 115, 116, 141n35
"alien citizenship," 24
Althusser, Louis, 49–50, 134n13
ambiguity, 44, 45, 94; and access to education, 6, 8, 42, 46, 57, 64; adaptation process (migration), 71, 72; and ambivalence, 78, 86; legal gaps, 60; legal opacity, 51, 53, 56, 86, 89, 143n4; and membership, 65; social exclusion, 3, 7, 46, 111, 116–117, 137n43; structural invisibility, 3, 4, 8, 57, 112, 116–117; and subjection, 52
ambivalence: concept of, 140n27; dynamics of, 8; forms of, 3, 6, 112, 118; living with, 7, 64, 76–77, 78, 86; production of, 3, 12, 14, 77, 112; recognition, 110–113; rejection of, 97; with relationships, 11–12, 76–77, 78, 79, 140n25, 140n26; unspoken, 53
*A.M.R.I. v. K.E.R.* (2001), 31
Anzaldúa, Gloria, 77–78
Arendt, Hannah, 24, 119
arrest, 32, 43, 80, 92, 110, 143n4
asylum: claims, 19, 21–22, 31, 85, 99, 110; policies, 130n12; refusal, 22, 42, 56, 100; seekers, 45, 59, 109, 146n2, 146n4

attachments, social, 29, 70, 71, 73, 79, 138n14. *See also* belonging

*Baker v. Canada* (1999), 22–24, 26, 130n22
Basso, Keith, 70–71
Bateson, Gregory, 91–92, 145n27, 145n28
belonging: ambivalent, 2–3, 8–12, 75–76, 78–79, 128n50; creation of, 8–9, 10, 98–100, 103; definition, 10, 71, 72–73; and deportability, 65, 68; effects of undocumented status, 7, 8, 15, 16, 64–65, 74; politics of, 72, 74, 139n15; recognition, 41, 73; spaces of, 70, 71; theorizations of, 75, 77
best interests of children: dependency, 23, 24–25, 26, 33, 131n29; protection, 20, 22
Bhabha, Homi, 76, 140n27, 140n29, 141n35
Bhabha, Jacqueline, 5, 24, 115
*Billy Budd* (Melville), 86, 87
border crossings: media coverage, 8, 146n2; nightmares about, 80–81, 82; trauma, 35, 80, 85; vulnerability, 83, 86, 143n4
boyfriends, 61–62, 63, 74
bureaucracy (access to education), 46, 56, 58, 69; use of discretion, 57, 58, 136n30, 136n36. *See also* school administration
bureaucratic disentitlement, 47
Butler, Judith, 21, 49, 50, 87, 111, 142n2

Canadian-born children, 23–25, 130n21
Canadian Charter of Rights and Freedoms, 32, 131n29
Canadian government, 20, 49, 73, 86, 99, 102

# ABOUT THE AUTHOR

FRANCESCA MELONI is assistant professor of social justice at King's College London.

# Available titles in the
# Rutgers Series in Childhood Studies

Laura Moran, *Belonging and Becoming in a Multicultural World: Refugee Youth and the Pursuit of Identity*

Hannah Dyer, *The Queer Aesthetics of Childhood: Asymmetries of Innocence and the Cultural Politics of Child Development*

Julie Spray, *The Children in Child Health: Negotiating Young Lives and Health in New Zealand*

Franziska Fay, *Disputing Discipline: Child Protection, Punishment, and Piety in Zanzibar Schools*

Kathie Carpenter, *Life in a Cambodian Orphanage: A Childhood Journey for New Opportunities*

Norbert Ross, *A World of Many: Ontology and Child Development among the Maya of Southern Mexico*

Camilla Morelli, *Children of the Rainforest: Shaping the Future in Amazonia*

Junehui Ahn, *Between Self and Community: Children's Personhood in a Globalized South Korea*

Francesca Meloni, *Ways of Belonging: Undocumented Youth in the Shadow of Illegality*

Printed and bound by CPI Group (UK) Ltd, Croydon, CR0 4YY

09/06/2025

14685729-0001

.